A quick beginners' course
in spoken Russian for
holidaymakers and business
people

Course writer
Nicholas J. Brown
Lecturer in Russian
School of Slavonic
and East European Studies
University of London

Producer: Philippa Goodrich

BBC Books

Get by in Russian
A BBC Radio course
First broadcast in Spring 1990

Published to accompany a series of programmes
prepared in consultation with the Continuing Education
Advisory Council

Acknowledgments
The author is grateful for the assistance of Keith Crawford,
Vanessa Daubney, Kathy Flower, Philippa Goodrich, Sarah
Hoggett and Suzanne Webber at the BBC; and to Irina Panasyuk,
Galya, Gena, Lena, Lyosha, Misha, Sasha, Margarita Yakovlyevna
and some two hundred other native speakers of Russian.

Illustrations by Peter Clark

Published by BBC Books, a division of BBC Enterprises Ltd,
Woodlands, 80 Wood Lane, London W12 0TT

ISBN 0 563 36474 2
First published in 1990
This edition published in 1993
Reprinted 1994
© Nicholas J. Brown 1990, 1993

Printed in England by Clays Ltd, St Ives plc
This book is set in 10 and 11 point Helvetica by Typesetters Ltd,
Hertford, Hertfordshire

Contents

RUSSIA

Scale: 1cm = 700kms

RUSSIA AND NEIGHBOURING STATES WITH THEIR CAPITALS

① **Russia**	**Moscow**	
② Ukraine	Kiev	
③ Belarus	Minsk	
④ Kazakhstan	Alma-Ata	
⑤ Uzbekistan	Tashkent	
⑥ Turkmenistan	Ashkhabad	
⑦ Estonia	Tallinn	
⑧ Latvia	Riga	
⑨ Lithuania	Vilnius	
⑩ Moldova	Chişinău	
⑪ Georgia	Tbilisi	
⑫ Azerbaijan	Baku	
⑬ Armenia	Yerevan	
⑭ Kyrgyzstan	Bishkek	
⑮ Tajikistan	Dushanbe	

About 'Get by in Russian'

Get by in Russian is a basic 'survival kit' to help you manage without your tour guide and let you get away from the English-only tourist track. The book can be used on its own, but for best results you need the accompanying two cassettes.

Most of the conversations were specially recorded in Moscow and St Petersburg (Leningrad) – in streets, flats, shops, hotels and cafés – so that you get used to hearing authentic Russian right from the start.

The Russian (Cyrillic) alphabet may seem a daunting hurdle at first, but you will find that learning it is an important part of 'getting by'. In Russia street signs, station names, notices and so on are written only in Russian letters. In this book we give Russian words in both Cyrillic and English letters but we recommend that you try to get used to reading Cyrillic as soon as possible.

Welcome to Russia

Russia is by far the largest country in the world. It is one-eighth of the world's land surface, twice the size of China, seventy times the size of Great Britain. European Russia, which is west of the Ural Mountains and contains the famous cities of Moscow and St Petersburg, is the best-known part, but most of the country is in Asia. Just as America once had a 'Wild West', Russia has a 'Wild East', the vast thinly populated expanses of Siberia. Many different nationalities speaking a wide variety of languages are intermixed across the 11 000 kilometres of Russian territory, but the vast majority of the population of 150 million are ethnic Russians.

The country is so big that Muscovites are having breakfast while their compatriots on the Kamchatka peninsula in the Far East are sitting down to their evening meal, ten hours ahead. The world's greatest train journey, the Trans-Siberian from Moscow to Vladivostok on the Sea of Japan, takes nearly a week.

To Westerners, Russia, part European, part Asian, was for centuries a remote and backward place. Although the Russian Empire of the tsars started to industrialise at the end of the nineteenth century, the country was a very long way behind Britain, France and Germany when the February and October revolutions of 1917 swept away the monarchy and the social order described in the works of Chekhov and Tolstoy and led to the creation of the Soviet Union. From the misery and defeat of the First World War, Russia was plunged into the upheavals of Lenin's Communist experiment, the trauma of the 1918-20 Civil War, then the years of Stalin's ruthless dictatorship and the holocaust of Hitler's 1941 invasion. After 1945 the European part of the country had to be rebuilt, while the 'Cold War' between the 'Iron Curtain' Communist countries of Eastern Europe and the Western democracies was used to justify severe restrictions on individual freedom, huge expenditure on arms and space rockets, and a low standard of living for most of the population. Only in the late 1980s, after 40 years of peace and 35 years since the end of Stalin's reign of terror, did the Soviet Union's leaders begin to feel secure enough to relax the repressive regime in the hope of improving both living standards and the country's image abroad. Mikhail Sergeevich Gorbachev, who became General Secretary of the Soviet Communist Party and thus leader of the country in 1985, introduced political and economic reforms which eventually acquired a momentum of their own, finally sweeping away the whole Communist system in a remarkable, peaceful revolution in 1991. The other fourteen republics of the former Soviet Union broke away from Russia, which, vast, still powerful and potentially rich, is rediscovering its own pre-Communist past and looking for a new role in world affairs.

Western visitors, despite the momentous changes of the last few years, still tend to find Russia rather drab on the surface. However, they always comment on the friendliness of the Russians, their love of parties (not political ones), and their eagerness to meet foreigners. Despite their revolutions, the Russians always give the impression of being a conservative people who believe in such things as stability, family life, entertaining friends at home and a sense of community. They are very proud of their language and its world-class literature. Despite 1917 and the Communists, twentieth-century Russian is in all essentials the same language as Dostoevsky and Chekhov used a hundred years ago. You will also find a great deal of uniformity across Russia: dialect variations are surprisingly small for such a large country and will not cause the foreign learner problems.

The Russian (Cyrillic) Alphabet

The Cyrillic alphabet was invented around 860 AD, possibly by St Cyril, a Macedonian monk. It is based on Greek.

To 'get by' in Russian – to read signs and street names, for example – you will need to know this alphabet. It is not difficult to learn and, apart from some minor exceptions (see page 12), words are pronounced as they are written. In this book all the Cyrillic in the first three units is also given in English letters; in the other three units, all new words are given in both Cyrillic and English letters, as are parts of the dialogues, so that you can check your pronunciation and progress. To make things easier, when showing the pronunciation in English letters, we have also divided the words up into syllables.

We'll do the five easy letters first:

CAPITAL	SMALL	PRONUNCIATION
A	a	a as in father
K	к	k as in kangaroo
M	м	m as in man
T	т	t as in tan
O	o	o as in bottle (*but* pronounced a when unstressed, i.e. with no stress mark '; see page 12)

Examples

так	[tak]	'so'
там	[tam]	'there'
как	[kak]	'how'
кто́-то	[któ-ta]	'somebody'

Then the seven letters which look like English letters but have different sounds:

В	в	v as in vet
Е	е	ye as in yes
Н	н	n as in never
Р	р	r as in error (rolled as in Scots English)
С	с	s as in sit
У	у	oo as in boot
Х	х	h pronounced like the ch in Scots loch or German Bach

Examples

нет	[nyet]	no
Москва́	[Mask-vá]	Moscow
метро́	[mye-tró]	metro, underground
Ве́ра	[Vyé-ra]	Vera
вам	[vam]	to you
у́тро	[óo-tra]	morning
о́н	[ón]	he
она́	[a-ná]	she
сестра́	[sye-strá]	sister
рестора́н	[rye-sta-rán]	restaurant
са́хар	[sá-har]	sugar

Next, 13 letters which look unfamiliar but have familiar sounds:

Б	б	b as in bet
Г	г	g as in get
Д	д	d as in debt
Ё	ё	yo as in yonder
З	з	z as in zoo
И	и	ee as in eel
Й	й	y as in boy
Л	л	l as in people
П	п	p as in pet
Ф	ф	f as in fat
Э	э	e as in fed
Ю	ю	yoo as in universe
Я	я	ya as in yak

Examples

Аэрофло́т	[A-e-ra-flót]	Aeroflot
Байка́л	[Bay-kál]	Lake Baikal
где	[gdye]	where
да	[da]	yes
до свида́ния	[da-svee-dá-nee-ya]	goodbye
алло́	[a-lló]	hello (on phone)
и́ли	[ée-lee]	or
кио́ск	[kee-ósk]	kiosk
Ле́нин	[Lyé-neen]	Lenin
парк	[park]	park
Пра́вда	[Práv-da]	'Pravda'/truth
Росси́я	[Ra-ssée-ya]	Russia
телефо́н	[tye-lye-fón]	telephone
ко́фе	[kó-fye]	coffee
футбо́л	[foot-ból]	football
Югосла́вия	[Yoo-ga-slá-vee-ya]	Yugoslavia
я не зна́ю	[ya nye zná-yoo]	I don't know

Lastly, we have eight letters which take a little longer to learn:

Ж	ж	zh pronounced like the s in pleasure
Ц	ц	ts as in its
Ч	ч	ch as in check
Ш	ш	sh as in shall
Щ	щ	shsh as in Welsh sheep (longer and softer than **ш**)
Ъ	ъ	a rare letter, called the hard sign, which sounds like a very brief pause
Ы	ы	i as in bit, but with the tip of the tongue a little further back
Ь	ь	y as in canyon. This letter, called the soft sign, combines with the consonant to its left and makes it soft. So **нь**

sounds like the ny in ca<u>ny</u>on, with the [n] and [y] pronounced simultaneously. Always pronounce it like the 'y' in ca<u>ny</u>on, never as the 'y' in 'd<u>ye</u>'.

Examples

дру́жба	[dro̒ozh-ba]	friendship
гости́ница	[ga-ste̒e-nee-tsa]	hotel
чай	[chay]	tea
большо́й	[baly-shóy]	big
борщ	[borshsh]	beetroot soup
объявле́ние	[ab-ya-vlyé-nee-ye]	announcement
сын	[sin]	son
есть	[yesty]	there is
пять	[pyaty]	five
ваш	[vash]	your
щи	[shshee]	cabbage soup

Exercise 1

Practise reading the following words, which you will meet again in the units and which contain all the letters except the rare hard sign ъ. Listen to the cassette and check your pronunciation in the answers at the end of the book.

спаси́бо	'thank you'
два ко́фе	'two coffees'
четы́ре	'four'
я слу́шаю	'I'm listening'
Где музе́й?	'Where's the museum?'
моро́женое	'ice cream'
Э́то хорошо́	'That's good'
о́н придёт	'he'll come'
това́рищ	'comrade'
двена́дцать	'twelve'

Stress

Almost all Russian words have a heavy stress on one syllable. For example, the name **Владимир** (Vladimir) is pronounced [Vla-dee-meer], with a heavy stress on the second syllable, like Belínda (not Bélinda). In this book the stress is marked ′ on Russian words, whether they are written in Cyrillic or in English letters. You should try to learn the place of the stress when you learn the word.

Except in dictionaries and books for foreigners, Russians do not print the stress, so you will often have to read words whose stress you do not know; the safest thing is to read them with no stress at all, syllable by syllable.

Differences between spelling and speaking

When Russian is spoken at normal speed you will notice some differences between spelling and pronunciation. Listen carefully to the cassettes and compare the Cyrillic spelling with our representation of the pronunciation in English letters.

The most obvious one is the pronunciation of unstressed **o** as [a].

óн   [ón]   he
онá   [a-ná]   she

The **уй** in the middle of **пожáлуйста** 'please' is often omitted, giving [pa-zhál-sta].

The first **в** in **Здрáвствуйте** 'Hello' is never pronounced, so it's [Zdrá-stvooy-tye];

Чтó 'what' is pronounced [shtó] (not [chtó]).

Sometimes, for example at the ends of words:

б	[b]	is pronounced	[p]
в	[v]	is pronounced	[f]
г	[g]	is pronounced	[k]
д	[d]	is pronounced	[t]
ж	[zh]	is pronounced	[sh]
з	[z]	is pronounced	[s]

Don't worry about trying to remember all of these.
You will not be misunderstood if you simply
pronounce words as they are written.

Exercise 2

Try reading these common signs, then compare
your pronunciation with the cassette and the
answers at the back of the book.

Sign	Translation
БАР	BAR
БУФЕ́Т	SNACKBAR
ГОСТИ́НИЦА	HOTEL
ЗАКРЫ́ТО	CLOSED
ЗА́НЯТО	OCCUPIED
ЗАПРЕЩЕНО́	FORBIDDEN
ИНТУРИ́СТ	INTOURIST
КА́ССА	CASHDESK/TICKET OFFICE
К СЕБЕ́	PULL
МЕ́СТО ДЛЯ КУРЕ́НИЯ	SMOKING PERMITTED HERE
НЕ КУРИ́ТЬ	NO SMOKING
ОТ СЕБЯ́	PUSH
ПАРИКМА́ХЕРСКАЯ	HAIRDRESSER/ BARBER
ПО́ЧТА	POST OFFICE
РАЗМЕ́Н	COIN CHANGER (machine in metro stations)
РЕМО́НТ	CLOSED FOR REPAIRS
РЕСТОРА́Н	RESTAURANT
СВОБО́ДНО	UNOCCUPIED/FREE
СТО́П	STOP
СТОЯ́НКА ТАКСИ́	TAXI STAND
ТУАЛЕ́Т	TOILET

Russian words in English letters ('transcription')

The letters in our transcription system are to be read as in English, but be careful with the following ones:

ee always as in meet
   [tak-sée] 'taxi'
i is like the i in bit but with the tongue tip a little further back
   [vi] 'you'
oo always as in boot
   [mye-nyóo] 'menu'
r is always rolled as in Scottish English
   [rye-sta-rán] restaurant
sh as in shut
   [vash] 'your'
   [baly-shóy] 'big'
shsh as in Welsh sheep – a long soft sh sound
   [bórshsh] 'beetroot soup'
ts as in its
   [stán-tsi-ya] 'metro station'
y after a consonant or at the beginning of a syllable is pronounced as in yes:
   [Dyá-dya Vá-nya] 'Uncle Vanya'
   [yesty] 'there is'
   [nyet] 'no'
   After a vowel, pronounce it as in boy
   [móy] 'my'
   [moo-zyéy] 'museum'
   [Dáy-tye] 'Give!'
zh is pronounced like s in pleasure
   [pa-zhál-sta] 'please'

1 Greetings

Key expressions

Hello	**Здра́вствуйте** [Zdrá-stvooy-tye – the first **в** is *not* pronounced] **Здра́вствуй** [Zdrá-stvooy – used when speaking to a close friend or child]
Goodbye	**До свида́ния** [Da svee-dá-nee-ya]
Please (also 'Don't mention it', replying to 'Thank you')	**Пожа́луйста** [Pa-zhál-sta] (Note the unstressed <u>o</u> pronounced as [a])
Thank you	**Спаси́бо** [Spa-se͞e-ba]
1	**оди́н** [a-de͞en]
2	**два** [dva]
3	**три** [tree]
4	**четы́ре** [chye-tí-rye]

Conversations

1 Saying hello

MAN   **Здра́вствуйте!**[1]*
[Zdrá-stvooy-tye]

WOMAN   **Здра́вствуйте!**
[Zdrá-stvooy-tye]

* See the Explanations section.

2 Two friends say hello

SASHA   **Здра́вствуй[1], Лёша.**
[Zdrá-stvooy, Lyó-sha]

LYOSHA   **Здра́вствуй, Са́ша.**
[Zdrá-stvooy, Sá-sha]

3 Saying goodbye

MAN   **До свида́ния[2].**
[Da svee-dá-nee-ya]

WOMAN   **До свида́ния.**
[Da svee-dá-nee-ya]

4 Aspirin, please

CUSTOMER   **Аспири́н, пожа́луйста[3].**
[A-spee-re´en, pa-zhál-sta]

CHEMIST   **Пожа́луйста[3].**
[Pa-zhál-sta]

5 Saying thank you in a shop

CUSTOMER   **Спаси́бо[4].**
[Spa-se´e-ba]

ASSISTANT   **Пожа́луйста[3].**
[Pa-zhál-sta]

6 Ordering a coffee

WAITER   **Я вас слу́шаю.***
[Ya vas sló o-sha-yoo]

*This phrase is often used by waiters and shop assistants to show they are ready to serve you. It means literally, 'I'm listening to you'.

CUSTOMER	**Оди́н ко́фе, пожа́луйста.**
	[A-deé'en kó-fye, pa-zhál-sta]
WAITER	**Пожа́луйста.**
	[Pa-zhál-sta]

7 Ordering two coffees

WAITER	**Я вас слу́шаю.**
	[Ya vas sloó-sha-yoo]
CUSTOMER	**Два ко́фе, пожа́луйста.**
	[Dva kó-fye, pa-zhál-sta]
WAITER	**Пожа́луйста.**
	[Pa-zhál-sta]

8 Ordering four coffees

WAITER	**Я вас слу́шаю.**
	[Ya vas sloó-sha-yoo]
CUSTOMER	**Четы́ре ко́фе, пожа́луйста.**
	[Chye-tí-rye kó-fye, pa-zhál-sta]
WAITER	**Возьми́те, пожа́луйста.***
	[Vazy-meé'e-tye, pa-zhál-sta]

*Take (them), please.

9 Ordering a tea

WAITER	**Я вас слу́шаю.**
	[Ya vas sloó-sha-yoo]
CUSTOMER	**Оди́н чай, пожа́луйста.**
	[A-deé'en chay, pa-zhál-sta]
WAITER	**Пожа́луйста.**
	[Pa-zhál-sta]

Word List

ко́фе [kó-fye]	coffee
чай [chay]	tea
я [ya]	I
я (вас) слу́шаю	I'm listening (to you)
[ya (vas) sloó-sha-yoo]	

Explanations

1 Greetings

Здра́вствуйте [Zdrá-stvooy-tye] (literally, 'be healthy'). This is the commonest greeting at any time of day. It's a long word, probably the longest one you have to know in Russian, but you can use it to greet anybody, anywhere. Note that if the person you are speaking to is a friend, a child or a relative, you say

Здра́вствуй [Zdrá-stvooy]
without the final **-те** [-tye].

Good evening **До́брый ве́чер** [Dó-bri vyé-chyer]. You can use this from about 6 pm until midnight. **До́брый** [dó-bri] means 'good' or 'kind' and **ве́чер** [vyé-chyer] means 'evening'.

Good morning **До́брое у́тро** [Dó-bra-ye oó-tra]. As an alternative to **Здра́вствуйте**, you can use **До́брое у́тро** until midday. **У́тро** [oó-tra] means 'morning' and **до́брое** [dó-bra-ye] is a form of the word **до́брый** [dó-bri] ('good' or 'kind').

Good day **До́брый день** [Dó-bri dyeny]. You will also hear this alternative to **Здра́вствуйте**. **День** [dyeny] means 'day'. There is no Russian word for 'afternoon', so this is the one to use between midday and 6pm.

2 Goodbye

До свида́ния [da svee-dá-nee-ya]. Literally, this means 'until meeting'. The word **до** 'until' is usually pronounced without stress, which is why the letter o sounds like [a] (see the pronunciation guide on page 12).

3 Please/Don't mention it/Here you are/Please do

Пожа́луйста [pa-zhál-sta] or, in more careful speech, [pa-zhá-loo-sta].
If you decide to learn only half a dozen Russian words, make this word for 'please' one of them. Put

it in all your requests. Russians do not normally expect foreign visitors to know any Russian; use **пожа́луйста** and the stony-faced official might make an attempt at a smile.

Пожа́луйста also means 'Don't mention it' or 'You're welcome'. If someone says 'Thank you', **спаси́бо** [spa-se'e-ba], to you, you should reply **Пожа́луйста**, 'Don't mention it'. So the word for 'please' you learnt above is doubly useful.

You also use the word **пожа́луйста** when you give something to somebody ('Here you are') or give permission to do something ('Please do', 'Go ahead').

4 Thank you

Спаси́бо [spa-se'e-ba] is, of course, a vital word. It has religious origins: **спаси́** [spa-se'e] means 'save' and **бо** comes from **бог** [bok], 'God' – 'May God save (you)'. But it is now used by all Russians, atheists included, to mean 'thank you'.

Exercises

1   Reading practice

(b)

(d)

(e)

(f)

(g)

ПРАВДА
(h)

2 Say hello to **Ива́н Петро́вич** [Ee-ván Pye-tró-veech], whom you are meeting for the first time.

3 Say hello to your old friend Sasha (using the familiar form).

4 Play the part of the customer

WAITER	**Я вас слу́шаю.**
CUSTOMER	(Hello. Three coffees, please.)
WAITER	**Пожа́луйста.**
CUSTOMER	(Thank you)
WAITER	**Пожа́луйста.**
WAITER	**Я вас слу́шаю.**
CUSTOMER	(One tea, please)
WAITER	**Пожа́луйста.**
CUSTOMER	(Thank you)
WAITER	**Пожа́луйста.**

5 Read these words and check your pronunciation with the cassette:
(a) **оди́н, два, три, чай, ко́фе, четы́ре, спаси́бо, пожа́луйста, До́брый день, До́брое у́тро, До свида́ния, Здра́вствуйте.**
(b) **Москва́, во́дка, Ло́ндон, Чайко́вский, Достое́вский.**

(c) Here are some Russian names transcribed according to their pronunciation – do you recognise them? The traditional English spellings, and their Cyrillic spellings are given in the exercise key. [Tal-stóy], [Gar-ba-chyóf], [Pa-styer-nák], [Sal-zhe-née-tsin], [Hroo-shshyóf], [Póosh-keen], [Pra-kó-fyyef].

Worth knowing

Russian drinks

Everyone has heard of the strong Russian drink called **водка** [vót-ka], though few people know that its name comes from the word **вода** [va-dá] which means 'water'. Among non-alcoholic drinks, the most popular is of course **чай** [chay] 'tea', which is usually served in a thin glass held in a glass-holder (often decorated). An inch of very strong brew is poured into the glass from a small china teapot (**чайник** [cháy-neek]) and the glass is then filled with boiling water from a kettle or **самовар** [sa-ma-vár]. Samovars, which are water heaters, not teapots, traditionally used charcoal but modern ones are all electric.

No Russian ever puts milk in tea, but your glass (**стакан** [sta-kán]) may come with a slice of lemon (**с лимоном** [s lee-mó-nam] 'with lemon'). Lemons are, however, a luxury in Russia and most Russians simply flavour their tea with large lumps of slow-dissolving sugar. Sometimes in Russian homes the tea is accompanied by a small saucer of home-made jam (**варенье** [va-ryé-nyye]) which you eat with a spoon.

Coffee is also popular but very expensive. Ground or instant coffee makes a good present to take with you.

2 Buying things

Key expressions

Excuse (me)	**Простите** [Pra-stée-tye]
How much/How many	**Сколько** [Skóly-ka]
How much does it cost?	**Сколько стоит?** [Skóly-ka stó-eet?]
How much do they cost?	**Сколько стоят?** [Skóly-ka stó-yat?]
Could you repeat, please?	**Повторите, пожалуйста** [Pa-fta-rée-tye, pa-zhál-sta]
Show (me)	**Покажите** [Pa-ka-zhí-tye]
One rouble	**Один рубль** [A-deén roobly]
Two roubles	**Два рубля** [Dva roo-blyá]
Five roubles	**Пять рублей** [Pyaty roo-blyéy]
One kopeck	**Одна копейка** [Ad-ná ka-pyéy-ka]
Two kopecks	**Две копейки** [Dvye ka-pyéy-kee]
Five kopecks	**Пять копеек** [Pyaty ka-pyé-yek]
6	**шесть** [shesty]
7	**семь** [syemy]
8	**восемь** [vó-syemy]
9	**девять** [dyé-vyaty]
10	**десять** [dyé-syaty]

Thank you very much	**Спаси́бо большо́е**
	[Spa-see-ba baly-shó-ye]
Good/OK	**Хорошо́** [Ha-ra-shó]

Conversations

1 Counting to ten

CHILD   **Оди́н** [a-deén], **два** [dva], **три** [tree], **четы́ре** [chye-tí-rye], **пять** [pyaty], **шесть** [shesty], **семь** [syemy], **во́семь** [vó-syemy], **де́вять** [dyé-vyaty], **де́сять** [dyé-syaty].

2 Asking the price

CUSTOMER   **Ско́лько?**
[Skóly-ka]

ASSISTANT   **Со́рок пять[1]. Со́рок пять копе́ек[7].**
[Só-rak pyaty. Só-rak pyaty ka-pyé-yek]

CUSTOMER   **Спаси́бо большо́е.**
[Spa-see-ba baly-shó-ye]

ASSISTANT   **Пожа́луйста.**
[Pa-zhál-sta]

3 Asking how much it is

CUSTOMER   **Ско́лько э́то[2] сто́ит?**
[Skóly-ka é-ta stó-eet?]

TRADER   **Три́дцать пять.**
[Treé-tsaty pyaty]

CUSTOMER   **Спаси́бо.**
[Spa-see-ba]

4 How much is it?

CUSTOMER   **Ско́лько э́то сто́ит?**
[Skóly-ka é-ta stó-eet?]

TRADER   **Пятьдеся́т три копе́йки[6].**
[Pee-dye-syát tree ka-pyéy-kee]

5 How much are they?

CUSTOMER   **Ско́лько сто́ят?**
[Skóly-ka stó-yat?]

TRADER   **Три́дцать пять копе́ек.**
[Treé-tsaty pyaty ka-pyé-yek]

6   How much is one postcard?

CUSTOMER   **А ско́лько сто́ит одна́[4] откры́тка[3]?**
[A skóly-ka stó-eet ad-ná at-krít-ka?]

KIOSK LADY   **Шесть копе́ек.**
[Shesty ka-pyé-yek]

CUSTOMER   **Спаси́бо большо́е.**
[Spa-seé-ba baly-shó-ye]

7   Buying two envelopes for England

CUSTOMER   **Мне, пожа́луйста, два[5] конве́рта, самолётом.***
[Mnye, pa-zhál-sta, dva kan-vyér-ta, sa-ma-lyó-tam]

ASSISTANT   **Оди́н рубль две[5] копе́йки, пожа́луйста. Оди́н рубль две копе́йки.**
[A-deén roobly, dvye ka-pyéy-kee]

CUSTOMER   **Хорошо́.** [Ha-ra-shó]

* For me, please, two airmail envelopes. **Самолётом** means 'by plane'.

8   Buying two stamped postcards for England

CUSTOMER   **Здра́вствуйте.**

ASSISTANT   **Здра́вствуйте.**

CUSTOMER   **Мне, пожа́луйста, две откры́тки.**
[Mnye, pa-zhál-sta, dvye at-krít-kee]

ASSISTANT   **Две откры́тки – се́мьдесят копе́ек, пожа́луйста.** [Dvye at-krít-kee – syém-dye-syat ka-pyé-yek]

CUSTOMER   **Ско́лько? Повтори́те ещё раз.***
[Skóly-ka? Pa-fta-reé-tye ye-shshyó ras]

ASSISTANT   **Се́мьдесят. Се́мьдесят.**
[Syém-dye-syat]

CUSTOMER   **Спаси́бо.**

ASSISTANT   **Пожа́луйста. Пожа́луйста.**

* Repeat again.

9 Twenty envelopes and five postcards

ASSISTANT **Два́дцать конве́ртов[7] сто́ят рубль два́дцать. И пять откры́ток[7] сто́ят три́дцать копе́ек. Всего́ рубль пятьдеся́т.***
[Dvá-tsaty kan-vyér-taf stó-yat roobly dvá-tsaty. Ee pyaty at-krí-tak stó-yat treé-tsaty ka-pyé-yek. Fsye-vó roobly pee-dye-syát]

CUSTOMER **Прости́те, ско́лько?**
[Pra-steé-tye, skóly-ka?]

ASSISTANT **Рубль пятьдеся́т.**
[Roobly pee-dye-syát]

CUSTOMER **Спаси́бо.**

ASSISTANT **Пожа́луйста. Пожа́луйста.**

* Altogether (one) rouble fifty (kopecks).

10 Two stamped airmail envelopes

CUSTOMER **Здра́вствуйте, я хочу́ посла́ть письмо́ в А́нглию.*** Ско́лько э́то сто́ит?
[Ya ha-choó pa-sláty peesy-mó v Án-glee-yoo. Skóly-ka é-ta stó-eet?]

ASSISTANT **Пятьдеся́т одна́ копе́йка.**
[Pee-dye-syát ad-ná ka-pyéy-ka]

CUSTOMER **Два конве́рта, пожа́луйста.**
[Dva kan-vyér-ta, pa-zhál-sta]

ASSISTANT **Так, пожалуйста. Рубль две.**
[Tak, pa-zhál-sta. Roobly dvye]

* Hello, I want to send a letter to England.

11 Asking prices in the hotel shop

CUSTOMER **Ско́лько сто́ит во́дка?**
[Skóly-ka stó-eet vót-ka?]

ASSISTANT **Столи́чная во́дка пять рубле́й де́сять копе́ек. Пять де́сять.**
[Sta-leéch-na-ya vót-ka pyaty roo-blyéy dyé-syaty ka-pyé-yek. Pyaty dyé-syaty]

CUSTOMER **А ско́лько сто́ит Пе́пси-Ко́ла?**
[A skóly-ka stó-eet Pép-see-Kó-la?]

ASSISTANT **Пе́пси-Ко́ла сто́ит со́рок пять копе́ек.**
[Pép-see-Kó-la stó-eet só-rak pyaty ka-pyé-yek]

12 An amenable market trader selling pears

CUSTOMER **Ско́лько сто́ят ва́ши гру́ши?**
[Skóly-ka stó-yat vá-shi gró̱o-shi?]

TRADER **Пятна́дцать рубле́й.**
[Peet-ná-tsaty roo-blyéy]

CUSTOMER **А е́сли за де́сять рубле́й?***
[A yé-slee za dyé-syaty roo-blyéy?]

TRADER **Мо́жно**. Мо́жно, мо́жно, мо́жно.**
[Mózh-na]

* What if I offer ten?
** It's possible (=OK).

13 But this apple seller is less willing to bargain

CUSTOMER **Здра́вствуйте, ско́лько сто́ят ва́ши я́блоки?** [Skóly-ka stó-yat vá-shi yá-bla-kee?]

TRADER **Я́блоки сто́ят пять рубле́й килогра́мм.**
[Yá-bla-kee stó-yat pyaty roo-blyéy kee-la-grám]

CUSTOMER **Ой, э́то о́чень до́рого[8]. А за три рубля́?** [Óy, é-ta ó-chyeny dó-ra-ga. A za tree roo-blyá?]

TRADER **За три рубля́ нет.**
[Za tree roo-blyá nyet]

14 In many shops if you want to examine an item you must ask the assistant to show it to you

TOURIST **Покажи́те, пожа́луйста, вот э́то.***
[Pa-ka-zhí-tye, pa-zhál-sta, vót é-ta]

ASSISTANT **Э́то?** [É-ta?]

TOURIST **Нет** [Nyet]

ASSISTANT **Э́то?**

TOURIST **Да.** [Da]

ASSISTANT **Пожа́луйста.**

* Please show me that over there.

Word List

The word lists in the units give the words you should try to learn. Other words which occur in the conversations are in the full Russian–English list at the end of the book.

m=masculine; f=feminine; n=neuter

a [a]	but/and (slight contrast)
ва́ши [vá-shi]	your
во́т [vót]	here is/there is
да [da]	yes
до́ллар [dó-lar]	dollar
до́рого [dó-ra-ga]	expensive
е́сли [yé-slee]	if
за [za]	for
и [ee]	and
кило́ (n) [kee-ló]	kilo
килогра́мм (m) [kee-la-grám]	kilogram
конве́рт (m) [kan-vyért]	envelope
мне [mnye]	for me/to me
мо́жно [mózh-na]	it's possible
нет [nyet]	no
откры́тка (f) [at-krít-ka]	postcard
о́чень [ó-chyeny]	very
письмо́ (n) [peesy-mó]	letter
повтори́те [pa-fta-ree-tye]	repeat
скажи́те [ska-zhí-tye]	tell (me)
Столи́чная (f) [Sta-leéch-na-ya]	Stolichnaya (brand of vodka)
так [tak]	so
э́то [é-ta]	this/that/it
я хочу́ [ya ha-chóo]	I want

Explanations

1 Numbers 11-100

You already know the numbers from 1 to 10 (see page 22). The teens are formed by putting 1 to 9, sometimes with small spelling changes, in front of **на** [na] 'on' and **дцать** [tsaty], a form of **де́сять** 'ten':

11	**оди́ннадцать**	[a-de'e-na-tsaty]	= 'one on ten'
12	**двена́дцать**	[dvye-ná-tsaty]	= 'two on ten'
13	**трина́дцать**	[tree-ná-tsaty]	
14	**четы́рнадцать**	[chye-tír-na-tsaty]	
15	**пятна́дцать**	[peet-ná-tsaty]	
16	**шестна́дцать**	[shes-ná-tsaty]	
17	**семна́дцать**	[syem-ná-tsaty]	
18	**восемна́дцать**	[va-syem-ná-tsaty]	
19	**девятна́дцать**	[dye-veet-ná-tsaty]	

The numbers 20, 30, 50 and so on are made up in a similar way, but with no **на**; 40 and 90 are exceptions:

20	**два́дцать**	[dvá-tsaty]	'two ten'
30	**три́дцать**	[tre'e-tsaty]	'three ten'
40	**со́рок**	[só-rak]	
50	**пятьдеся́т**	[pee-dye-syát]	'five ten'
60	**шестьдеся́т**	[shez-dye-syát]	
70	**се́мьдесят**	[syém-dye-syat]	
80	**во́семьдесят**	[vó-syem-dye-syat]	
90	**девяно́сто**	[dye-vee-nó-sta]	

100	**сто́**	[stó]

Compound numbers (21, 49 etc.) are formed as in English:

21 = 20 (**два́дцать**) + 1 (**оди́н**) [dvá-tsaty a-de'en]: **два́дцать оди́н**

42 **со́рок два** [só-rak dva]

137 **сто́ три́дцать семь** (NB no 'and')

2 It/this/that

Это [É-ta] is the word to use when you don't know what something is called. It means 'it', 'this' and also 'that'.

What does it/this/that cost? **Сколько это стоит?** [Skóly-ka é-ta stó-eet?]

3 Gender of nouns

Russian nouns (words for things like 'envelope', 'postcard', 'letter') are masculine (m), feminine (f) or neuter (n). Words that end with a consonant, e.g. **конверт** [kan-vyért] 'envelope', are masculine; if the last letter is -a, the word is feminine, e.g. **открытка** [at-krít-ka] 'postcard'; the small number of nouns ending in -o are neuter, e.g. **письмо** [peesy-mó] 'letter'. Nouns ending with other letters are less predictable; the gender is shown in the word list in each unit.

4 One

The word for 'one' is

один [a-deén] with masculine words
одна [ad-ná] with feminine ones
одно [ad-nó] with neuter ones

один конверт [a-deén kan-vyért] one envelope
одна открытка [ad-ná at-krit-ka] one postcard
одно письмо [ad-nó peesy-mó] one letter

The same forms are used with compound numbers ending 'one' (21, 31, etc), and the noun is always *singular*:

пятьдесят одна копейка fifty-one kopecks [pee-dye-syát ad-ná ka-pyéy-ka] (literally 'fifty-one kopeck')
двадцать один рубль twenty-one roubles (literally 'twenty-one rouble')

5 Two

Two is **два** [dva] with masculine and neuter nouns, **две** [dvye] with feminine ones.
Рубль [roobly], the Russian unit of currency, is masculine:

Два рубля́ [dva roo-blyá] 'two roubles'

Копе́йка [ka-pyéy-ka], 'kopeck', one hundredth of a rouble, is feminine:
Две копе́йки [dvye ka-pyéy-kee] 'two kopecks'

The same applies to compound numbers ending in 'two' (22, 142 etc.)
Два́дцать два рубля́ 'twenty-two roubles'
[Dvá-tsaty dva roo-blyá]

6 Two, three, four of something

You may have noticed that in the last example **рубль** [roobly] became **рубля́** [roo-blyá] and **копе́йка** became **копе́йки** [ka-pyéy-kee]. This is because Russian is an inflected language, which means the endings of words change depending on the grammar of the sentence.

After the numbers two, three and four, nouns have an ending (called the genitive singular) which means 'of':
'Two/three/four roubles' is **два/три/четы́ре рубля́** [dva/tree/chye-tí-rye roo-blyá], meaning literally 'two/three/four of rouble'.
'Three kopecks' is **три копе́йки** [tree ka-pyéy-kee], which means 'three of kopeck'.

You find the same forms after 22, 23, 24 and all higher numbers ending 2, 3, 4:
со́рок два рубля́ 42 roubles [só-rak dva roo-blyá]

7 Five, six, seven...

After five and larger numbers, Russian uses another ending. **Рубль** becomes **рубле́й** [roo-blyéy], which means 'of roubles', and **копе́йка** becomes **копе́ек** [ka-pyé-yek] 'of kopecks'. This ending is called the genitive plural.

Here are some more examples of things you may want to count:
одна́ откры́тка [ad-ná at-krít-ka]   1 postcard
три откры́тки [tree at-krít-kee]   3 postcards

пять откры́ток [pyaty at-krí-tak]   5 postcards

оди́н конве́рт [a-de'en kan-vyért]   1 envelope
два конве́рта [dva kan-vyér-ta]   2 envelopes
шесть конве́ртов [shesty kan-vyér-taf]
   6 envelopes

оди́н до́ллар [a-de'en dó-lar]   1 dollar
два до́ллара [dva dó-la-ra]   2 dollars
де́сять до́лларов [dyé-syaty dó-la-raf]   10 dollars

Don't worry about the details of these endings at
this stage. Learning Russian grammar is a big job,
but, fortunately, you don't need much to 'get by'. In
this book we'll try not to overburden you.

8   That is very expensive

Э́то о́чень до́рого [É-ta ó-chyeny dó-ra-ga]
'That very expensive'. Russian does not require any
equivalent of 'is', 'am', 'are'.

Exercises

1   What is the price?

CUSTOMER   Ско́лько э́то сто́ит?
TRADER   Четы́ре до́ллара. Четы́ре до́ллара.

2   How much must the customer pay?

ASSISTANT   Э́то сто́ит со́рок копе́ек.
CUSTOMER   Со́рок копе́ек? Пожа́луйста.

3   In the shop

(a) Ask how much it costs.
(b) Ask the assistant to give you three.
(c) Tell the cashier that you have to pay two roubles
   ten kopecks.

4   Play the part of the customer

CUSTOMER   (Ask how much a postcard costs)
ASSISTANT   Шесть копе́ек.
CUSTOMER   (Ask for two)
ASSISTANT   Пожа́луйста, двена́дцать копе́ек.
CUSTOMER   (Say thank you)
ASSISTANT   Пожа́луйста.

5 Play the part of the customer

CUSTOMER   (Ask the price of the apples)
TRADER   Пятна́дцать рубле́й килогра́мм.
CUSTOMER   (Offer eight)
TRADER   Нет. Двена́дцать.
CUSTOMER   (Offer ten)
TRADER   Оди́ннадцать.
CUSTOMER   (Accept eleven)
TRADER   Хорошо́. Ско́лько кило́?
CUSTOMER   (Say one kilogramme)

6 How much do you owe?

Со́рок четы́ре копе́йки.

7 How much do you owe?

Шестьдеся́т шесть копе́ек. Шестьдеся́т шесть.

8 What do the signs say?

(a)

(b)

(c)

Worth knowing

Shopping in Russia

Shopping is not likely to be the highlight of your Russian trip. Although the variety of shops and the range of goods has improved since the demise of communism, Russian quality is generally not up to Western standards and most things worth buying are Western imports. Apart from the obvious souvenirs such as the nested wooden dolls called **матрёшки** [ma-tryósh-kee], decorated boxes, **шкатулки** [shka-tóol-kee], and flavoured vodka, e.g. **перцовка** [pyer-tsóf-ka] 'pepper vodka', the best local buys are probably caviare (**икра** [ee-krá]), books (particularly glossy art books) and fur hats.

If you are shopping for food, there are supermarkets where you can simply take things off the shelves and pay for them at the check-out without saying a word. In some shops you can simply point at what you want and pay the assistant. But in many shops, before you receive goods you must pay for them at a cash desk some distance from the counter where they are sold. This means you may have to list your intended purchases and their prices to the cashier without being able to point at them. You decide what you want to buy, note the price, queue at the cash desk, tell the cashier what you want and he, or usually, she gives you a receipt (**чек** [chyek]) for each item. You take these **чеки** to the relevant counters and hand them over for the goods.

The best fruit, vegetables and meat are to be found in the private markets (**рынок** [rí-nak] 'market'), where prices are generally higher than in the shops. Sometimes there is room for bargaining.

Money in Russia

The Russian unit of currency is the rouble (**рубль** [roobly]), which is divided into one hundred kopecks (**копейка** [ka-pyéy-ka]). However, the preferred means of exchange for an increasing number of transactions is the US dollar; hotels, bars and shops for foreigners work almost exclusively in dollars, and many street traders and taxi drivers also insist on dollars. In hotels, restaurants and foreign-currency shops you can use Western credit cards, but you should take plenty of low-denomination dollar bills with you for everyday expenses. Pounds, German marks and other 'hard' currencies will not be refused, but you will get a better price if you use dollars.

Since 1991, the Russian economy has suffered from serious inflation. The rouble prices in the conversations in Units 2 and 3 are likely to be much lower than the ones you will meet in Russia. You may find that you need to add the following high numbers to the list on page 28:

200 двести [dvyé-stee]
300 триста [trée-sta]
400 четыреста [chye-tí-rye-sta]
500 пятьсот [peet-sót]
600 шестьсот [shes-sót]
700 семьсот [syem-sót]
800 восемьсот [va-syem-sót]
900 девятьсот [dye-veet-sót]
1000 тысяча [tí-sya-chya]

3 Food and Drink

Key expressions

Is there	**Есть?** [Yesty?]
Is there coffee?	**Есть кóфе?** [Yesty kó-fye?]
Have you got...?	**У вас есть...?** [Oo vas yesty...?]
Have you any beer?	**У вас есть пи́во?** [Oo vas yesty peé-va?]
What have you got?	**Чтó у вас есть?** [Shtó oo vas yesty?]
There isn't any Pepsi	**Пéпси нет** [Pép-see nyet]
Big	**Большóй** [Baly-shóy]
Small	**Мáленький** [Má-lyeny-kee]
With sugar	**С сáхаром** [Ssá-ha-ram]
Without sugar	**Без сáхара** [Byes sá-ha-ra]
A cheese sandwich	**Бутербрóд с сы́ром** [Boo-tyer-brót ssi-ram]
A bottle of mineral water, please	**Буты́лку минерáльной воды́, пожáлуйста** [Boo-tíl-koo mee-nye-rály-nay va-dí, pa-zhál-sta]
The bill, please	**Счёт, пожáлуйста** [Shshyot, pa-zhál-sta]

Conversations

1 Have you any coffee?

MAN **У вас есть[1,2] кóфе?**
[Oo vas yesty kó-fye?]

SNACKBAR GIRL **Да, есть.[3]**
[Da, yesty]

MAN **Два кóфе[4], пожáлуйста.**
[Dva kó-fye, pa-zhál-sta]

2 Big or small, with or without sugar?

GIRL **Вам большóй úли мáленький?**
[Vam baly-shóy ée-lee má-lyeny-kee?]

MAN **Большóй.**

GIRL **С сáхаром[6]?**
[Ssá-ha-ram?]

MAN **Да, с сáхаром, пожáлуйста.**

3 Open sandwiches and a drink.

GIRL **Я вас слýшаю.**

CUSTOMER **У вас есть бутербрóды?***
[Oo vas yesty boo-tyer-bró-di?]

GIRL **С колбасóй[6] и с сýром.**
[Skal-ba-sóy ee ssír-am]

CUSTOMER **Я не знáю[7]. С колбасóй – два. И два с сýром.**
[Ya nye zná-yoo. Skal-ba-sóy – dva. Ee dva ssí-ram]

GIRL **Пожáлуйста. А что вы бýдете пить?****
[A shtó vi boo-dye-tye peety?]

CUSTOMER **Пéпси, пожáлуйста.**

GIRL **Пéпси нет[5].**
[Pép-see nyet]

CUSTOMER **Тогдá пúво.**
[Tag-dá pée-va]

GIRL **Пúва тóже нет[5].**
[Pée-va tó-zhe nyet]

CUSTOMER **А чтó есть?**
[A shtó yesty?]

GIRL	**Со́к и минера́льная вода́.** [Sók ee mee-nye-rály-na-ya va-dá]
CUSTOMER	**Буты́лку[8] минера́льной воды́[9], пожа́луйста.** [Boo-tíl-koo mee-nye-rály-nay va-dí, pa-zhál-sta]

*Have you (any) sandwiches?
**And what will you drink?

4 What *have* you got to drink?

CUSTOMER	**Пи́во, пожа́луйста.** [Pée-va, pa-zhál-sta]
GIRL	**Пи́ва не́ту.** [Pée-va nyé-too]
CUSTOMER	**Вино́ есть?** [Vee-nó yesty?]
GIRL	**Нет.**
CUSTOMER	**А во́дка есть?** [A vót-ka yesty?]
GIRL	**То́же нет.** [Tó-zhe nyet]
CUSTOMER	**А что́ же у вас есть?*** [A shtó zhe oo vas yesty?]
GIRL	**Есть со́к и Пе́пси. Минера́льная вода́.** [Yesty sók ee Pép-see. Mee-nye-rály-na-ya va-dá]
CUSTOMER	**Како́й со́к?** [Ka-kóy sók?]
GIRL	**Апельси́новый.** [A-pyely-sée-na-vi]
CUSTOMER	**Оди́н, пожа́луйста.**
GIRL	**Пожа́луйста.**

*What *have* you got then? **же** [zhe] makes the question emphatic.

5 Ordering borshsh, a hamburger and ice cream

WAITER	**До́брый ве́чер. Во́т вам меню́, пожа́луйста.** [Dó-bri vyé-chyer. Vót vam mye-nyoó]

DINER	**Дóбрый вéчер. Борщ, пожáлуйста, и на втóрое блюдо бифштéкс. ***
	[Borshsh, pa-zhál-sta, ee na fta-ró-ye blyoó-da beef-shtéks]
WAITER	**Чтó вы бýдете на десéрт?****
	[Shtó vi boó-dye-tye na dye-syért?]
DINER	**На десéрт морóженое.**
	[Na dye-syért ma-ró-zhe-na-ye]
WAITER	**Однý минýту. *****
	[Ad-noó mee-noó-too]

* and for the main course a hamburger.

** What will you have for dessert?

*** Just a minute

6 Some wine

DINER	**А чтó у вас есть вы́пить?**
	[A shtó oo vas yesty ví-peety?]
WAITRESS	**Есть винó сухóе. Бéлое, крáсное. Какóе вы бýдете?***
	[Yesty vee-nó soo-hó-ye. Byé-la-ye, krá-sna-ye. Ka-kó-ye vi boó-dye-tye?]
DINER	**Пожáлуйста, бéлое винó.**
	[... byé-la-ye vee-nó]
WAITRESS	**Пожáлуйста.**

* What kind will you take?

7 A vegetarian

DINER	**Официáнт, бýдьте добры́. ***
	[A-fee-tsi-ánt, boó-tye da-brí]
WAITRESS	**Пожáлуйста, я вас слýшаю.**
DINER	**Я вегетариáнец.**
	[Ya vye-gye-ta-ree-á-nyets]
WAITRESS	**Вы бýдете есть ры́бу? ****
	[Vi boó-dye-tye yesty rí-boo?]
DINER	**Нет, я ем тóлько óвощи. *****
	[Nyet, ya yem tóly-ka ó-va-shshee]
WAITRESS	**Хорошó, я принесý для вас óвощи.******
	[Ha-ra-shó, ya pree-nye-soó dlya vas ó-va-shshee]

DINER   **Спасибо.**
WAITRESS   **Пожалуйста.**

* Waiter, excuse me (lit. 'be so good')
** Will you eat fish?
*** I eat only vegetables.
**** All right, I'll bring you (for you) vegetables.

8   The bill, please

DINER   **Официант. Счёт, пожалуйста.**
             [A-fee-tsi-ánt. Shshyot]
WAITRESS   **Пожалуйста, с вас* четыре рубля**
           девяносто пять копеек.
           [svas chye-tí-rye roo-blyá dye-vee-nó-sta
           pyaty ka-pyé-yek]
DINER   **Сколько, простите?**
             [Skóly-ka, pra-steé-tye?]
WAITRESS   **Четыре рубля девяносто пять**
           копеек.

* You owe (lit. 'from you').

Word list

апельсиновый сок (m)	orange juice
[a-pyely-seé-na-vi sók]	
без [byes]	without
белое вино (n)	white wine
[byé-la-ye vee-nó]	
бифштекс (m)	'beefsteak', meat
[beef-shtéks]	rissole, hamburger
большой [baly-shóy]	large
борщ (m) [bórshsh]	beetroot soup
бутерброд (m)	open sandwich
[boo-tyer-brót]	
бутылка (f) [boo-tíl-ka]	bottle
вам [vam]	to you/for you
вино (n) [vee-nó]	wine
вода (f) [va-dá]	water
водка (f) [vót-ka]	vodka
вот [vót]	here (pointing)
второе блюдо (n)	second course (main
[fta-ró-ye blyoó-da]	course)

на второе [na fta-ró-ye]	for the main course
вы́пить [ví-peety]	to drink (alcohol)
десе́рт (m) [dye-syért]	dessert
на десе́рт [na dye-syért]	for dessert
для [dlya]	for (somebody)
для вас [dlya vas]	for you
(я) ем [(ya) yem]	(I) eat
есть [yesty]	is/are
есть [yesty]	to eat
я зна́ю [ya zná-yoo]	I know
я не зна́ю [ya nye zná-yoo]	I don't know
и́ли [ée-lee]	or
како́й [ka-kóy]	what kind of
колбаса́ (f) [kal-ba-sá]	salami
с колбасо́й [skal-ba-sóy]	with salami
кра́сное вино́ (n) [krá-sna-ye vee-nó]	red wine
ма́ленький [má-lyeny-kee]	small
меню́ (n) [mye-nyoó]	menu
минера́льная вода́ (f) [mee-nye-rály-na-ya]	mineral water
моро́женое (n) [ma-ró-zhe-na-ye]	ice cream
нет [nyet]	there is no
не́ту [nyé-too] (coll.)	there is no
о́вощи (m) [ó-va-shshee]	vegetables
официа́нт (m) [a-fee-tsi-ánt]	waiter/waitress
пи́во (n) [pée-va]	beer
пить [peety]	to drink
ры́ба (f) [ri-ba]	fish
с [s]	with
с вас [svas]	from you
са́хар (m) [sá-har]	sugar
сок (m) [sók]	juice
сухо́е вино́ (n) [soo-hó-ye vee-nó]	dry wine
счёт (m) [shshyot]	bill

сыр (m) [sir]	cheese
с сы́ром [ssí-ram]	with cheese
тогда́ [tag-dá]	then
то́же [tó-zhe]	too
то́лько [tóly-ka]	only
у вас [oo vas]	you have
что́ [shtó]	what
что́ же [shtó zhe]	what (more emphatic)

Explanations

1 Is there...?/Are there...?

Есть [yesty] 'is'/'are' is used when you want to know if something is available:

Is there tea?	**Есть чай?**
Are there sandwiches?	**Есть бутербро́ды?**
Is there wine?	**Есть вино́?**
Is there any beer?	**Есть пи́во?**

The order of words is flexible. You can also say **Чай есть?**, **Вино́ есть?** etc.

If you have the cassette, listen to the voice rising on **есть** in these questions.

2 Have you got?

The same useful word **есть** occurs in the Russian construction for 'have':

У вас есть ко́фе?   Have you any coffee?
[Oo vas yesty kó-fye?]
This means literally 'By (**у**) you (**вас**) is (**есть**) coffee (**ко́фе**)?

Have you any sandwiches?   **У вас есть бутербро́ды?**

3 There is/there are

If something is available, you hear the same word, **есть**.

Да, есть	Yes, there is
Есть со́к и Пе́пси	There is juice and Pepsi

Вино́ есть?	Is there any wine?
Вино́ есть.	There is wine.

Notice that in spoken Russian, the difference between these two sentences is the voice rising on **есть** in the question.

4   Coffee and Pepsi: easy words

'Coffee', which we met in unit 1, is **ко́фе** [kó-fye], a masculine noun. 'Two coffees', or, as the Russians say, 'two of coffee', is **два ко́фе** [dva kó-fye]. You see that there is no change in the form of the word **ко́фе**. In fact, **ко́фе** never changes its form, regardless of grammar. Because of its foreign origin and (to a Russian) foreign sound, it doesn't obey the usual grammatical rules. The same is true of the foreign word **Пе́пси** [Pép-see].

5   There isn't any/aren't any

Нет (the same as the word for 'no') means 'there isn't' or 'there aren't'. There is also a colloquial form **не́ту** [nyé-too].

Ко́фе нет (or **Нет ко́фе**) means 'There's no coffee'
Пе́пси нет [Pép-see nyet] 'There's no Pepsi'
Пи́ва не́ту [Pée-va nyé-too] 'There's no beer'
Во́дки нет [Vót-kee nyet] 'There's no vodka'

You may have noticed the change in the ending of **пи́во** 'beer' and **во́дка** 'vodka' with **нет**. **Пи́ва** means 'of beer' and **во́дки** means 'of vodka'. In Russian, when **нет** means 'there isn't/aren't', nouns are put in a form called the *genitive*, which means 'of'. So **Во́дки нет** literally means 'There isn't of vodka'. **Ко́фе** and **Пе́пси** don't change their endings, as explained in 4 above.

6   With

After the short word **с** meaning 'with', Russian words add endings called the *instrumental case* (just a grammatical name). Here are some examples:

са́хар 'sugar';   **с са́харом** 'with sugar'
сыр 'cheese';   **с сы́ром** with cheese'
колбаса́ 'salami';   **с колбасо́й** 'with sausage'

7   I know/I don't know

Я зна́ю [Ya zná-yoo] is 'I know'. To make it negative, simply put **не** in front of **зна́ю**: **Я не зна́ю** [Ya nye zná-yoo] 'I don't know'.

8   (Bring me) a bottle

Буты́лку [boo-tíl-koo] is a form of the word **буты́лка** [boo-tíl-ka] 'bottle'. The ending of **буты́лку** is called the *accusative case* and is used to show the object of a verb, as opposed to the subject. The customer's phrase is short for *'Bring me* a bottle'. 'Bottle' is the object of the verb 'to bring' and so the accusative ending is used, just as in English we say, 'Bring her', not 'Bring she'. Russian nouns ending in **-a** all change the **-a** to **-y** in the accusative. Most other nouns don't change.

9   A bottle of mineral water

The 'of' in 'of something' corresponds to the Russian genitive case endings, the endings we met after **нет** 'there isn't' in 5 above. **Минера́льная вода́** 'mineral water' becomes **минера́льной воды́** [mee-nye-rály-nay va-dí] if you want to say 'of mineral water'.

Exercises

1   Read the following list of drinks, then listen to the real-life café dialogue and mark which of the drinks are available. There are some words you haven't met yet (they are in the key) but you should concentrate on recognising the words you've learnt so far.

минера́льная вода́	mineral water
во́дка	vodka

кófe без молокá	coffee without milk/black coffee
кófe с молокóм	coffee with milk/white coffee
Пéпси-Кóла	Pepsi-Cola
лимонáд [lee-ma-nát]	lemonade

A Скажи́те, пожа́луйста, у вас есть минера́льная вода́?
B Нет, минера́льной воды́ сего́дня нет.
A А скажи́те, пожа́луйста, у вас есть во́дка?
B Нет, у нас во́дки не быва́ет.
A Спаси́бо. А у вас есть сего́дня кóфе?
B Да, кófe есть. То́лько без молока́.
A А есть Пéпси-Кóла и́ли лимона́д?
B Есть лимона́д. Пéпси-Кóлы нет.
A Спаси́бо.

2 What does the customer decide to order?

CUSTOMER Я возьму́ ча́шку кófe.
WAITER Большо́й и́ли ма́ленький?
CUSTOMER Ма́ленький.
WAITER С са́харом?
CUSTOMER Да.
WAITER Два́дцать шесть копе́ек, пожа́луйста.

3 How much do you owe?

WAITER Вот вам счёт, пожа́луйста. С вас де́сять рубле́й со́рок копе́ек.

4 You are the customer

YOU (Waiter, the bill, please)
WAITER С вас де́вять рубле́й во́семь копе́ек.
YOU (Ask him to repeat)
WAITER Де́вять рубле́й во́семь копе́ек.

5 How much do you owe?

(a) С вас во́семь рубле́й три́дцать копе́ек.
(b) С вас пятьдеся́т копе́ек.
(c) С вас три рубля́ пятна́дцать копе́ек.
(d) С вас двена́дцать рубле́й во́семьдесят шесть копе́ек.

6 Play the part of the customer

YOU   (Excuse me, is there any coffee?)
WAITER   Ко́фе нет.
YOU   (Is there any vodka?)
WAITER   Во́дки то́же нет.
YOU   (Is there any tea?)
WAITER   Ча́я то́же нет.
YOU   (What have you got?)
WAITER   Есть Пе́пси, минера́льная вода́, лимона́д.
YOU   (Mineral water, please)
WAITER   Ско́лько буты́лок?*
YOU   (Two, please)
WAITER   Пожа́луйста, с вас се́мьдесят копе́ек.

* 'How many (of) bottles?'

Worth knowing

Russian restaurants

A Russian package tour includes all meals, and no choice of menu will be offered. The fare will be standard international, with a lot of chicken and beef. Bread, white and black, is served at all meals; breakfast may include one of the yogurt-type drinks such as **кефи́р** [kye-fe'er] or **простоква́ша** [pra-sta-kvá-sha]; lunch always includes soup. Mineral water (**минера́льная вода́**), tea (**чай**) and coffee (**ко́фе**), and sometimes beer (**пи́во**) will be brought automatically. The only Russian you will need is for special requests, such as vegetarian food. But be warned that Russians associate meat with the good life and find vegetarianism almost incomprehensible. Although hotel restaurants are getting used to foreign vegetarians and understand the implications of **Я вегетариа́нец** [Ya vye-gye-ta-ree-án-ets] (if you're a man) or **Я вегетариа́нка** [Ya vye-gye-ta-ree-án-ka] (if you're a woman), they will often just bring an omelette or the meat dish minus the meat (i.e. just the vegetables). There is little point in making a fuss about the dullness of this diet: vegetarian cooking is *not* part of Russian culture.

For real Russian cooking, you will have to get yourself invited to Russian homes (see Unit 6). To try non-Russian cooking, there are ethnic restaurants in Moscow, such as the Georgian **Ара́гви** [A-rág-vee], the Uzbek **Узбекиста́н** [Ooz-

МЕНЮ

АРАГВИ

bye-kee-stán] or the Armenian **Арме́ния** [Ar-myé-nee-ya]. To avoid lengthy queuing in the street, get your hotel Service Bureau to book you a table. The extensive menu will be in several languages, including English, but only those items which have prices are available. Your need for Russian will be minimal.

The spread of 'cooperative' or private restaurants means that the gastronomic scene is changing – and improving. So if you want a change from the unadventurous food of the package hotels and restaurants, get a Russian friend to take you to a cooperative (**кооперати́в** [ka-a-pye-ra-te'ef]). You pay the not inconsiderable bill, your friend will do the explaining and interpreting.

4 Getting around town

Key expressions

Tell me please	**Скажи́те, пожа́луйста** [Ska-zhí-tye]
Where is ...?	**Где ...?** [Gdye...?]
Red Square	**Кра́сная пло́щадь** [Krá-sna-ya pló-shshyaty]
On/to the left	**Нале́во** [Na-lyé-va]
On/to the right	**Напра́во** [Na-prá-va]
Straight on	**Пря́мо** [Pryá-ma]
Far	**Далеко́** [Da-lye-kó]
Not far	**Недалеко́** [Nye-da-lye-kó]
Round the corner	**За угло́м** [Za oo-glóm]
Along the street	**По у́лице** [Pa óo-lee-tse]
How do I get to the Russian Museum (on foot)?	**Как пройти́ в Ру́сский музе́й?** [Kak pray-teé v Róo-skee moo-zyéy?]
When do I get off?	**Когда́ выходи́ть?** [Kag-dá vi-ha-deéty?]
Are you getting off?	**Вы выхо́дите?** [Vi vi-hó-dee-tye?]
The next stop	**Сле́дующая остано́вка** [Slyé-doo-yoo-shsha-ya a-sta-nóf-ka]
At the next stop	**На сле́дующей остано́вке**
Pass (my ticket) along, please	**Переда́йте, пожа́луйста** [Pye-rye-dáy-tye]
I don't understand	**Я не понима́ю** [Ya nye pa-nee-má-yoo]

Conversations

1 Finding Tverskaya Street (Moscow's main street)

VISITOR **Скажи́те, пожа́луйста[1], где[2] Тверска́я у́лица?**
[Ska-zhi-tye, pa-zhál-sta, Tvyer-ská-ya gdye oó-lee-tsa?]

PASSER-BY **Пря́мо и напра́во.**
[Pryá-ma ee na-prá-va]

2 Where's Red Square, please?

TOURIST **Скажи́те, пожа́луйста, где Кра́сная пло́щадь?**
[Ska-zhi-tye, pa-zhál-sta, gdye Krá-sna-ya pló-shshyaty?]

MUSCOVITE **За угло́м и по у́лице, пря́мо.**
[Za oo-glóm ee pa oó-lee-tse, pryá-ma]

3 Where's the post office, please?

VISITOR **Прости́те, пожа́луйста, вы не зна́ете, где здесь по́чта?***
[Pra-stée-tye, pa-zhál-sta, vi nye zná-ye-tye, gdye zdyesy póch-ta?]

PASSER-BY **Зна́ю. Ря́дом. До́м шестьдеся́т два.****
[Zná-yoo. Ryá-dam. Dóm shez-dye-syát dva]

VISITOR **А где э́то?**
[A gdye é-ta?]

PASSER-BY **Во́т напра́во.*****
[Vót na-prá-va]

VISITOR **Спаси́бо большо́е.**

PASSER-BY **Пожа́луйста.**

* Do you know (=Don't you know) where the post office is here?
**I know. (It's) nearby. House (building) no. 62
***Over there on the right.

4 How do I get to the Russian Museum?
(The main museum in St Petersburg for paintings by Russian artists)

WOMAN **Скажи́те, пожа́луйста, как пройти́ в[4] Ру́сский музе́й?**
[Ska-zhi-tye, pa-zhál-sta, kak pray-tée v Roó-skee moo-zyéy?]

MAN	**Прямо и налево.**
	[Pryá-ma ee na-lyé-va]
WOMAN	**Спасибо.**
MAN	**Пожалуйста.**

5 How do I get there?

VISITOR	**Как проехать туда[3]?**
	[Kak pra-yé-haty too-dá?]
MUSCOVITE	**Надо сесть на автобус и проехать три остановки.***
	[Ná-da syesty na af-tó-boos ee pra-yé-haty tree a-sta-nóf-kee]
VISITOR	**Спасибо.**
MUSCOVITE	**Пожалуйста.**
VISITOR	**До свидания.**

*You have to take a bus and travel three stops.

6 How do I get to the Hermitage?
(St Petersburg's most famous museum)

MAN	**Добрый день. Скажите, пожалуйста, где Эрмитаж?**
	[Dó-bri dyeny. Ska-zhí-tye, pa-zhál-sta, gdye Er-mee-tásh?]
WOMAN	**Добрый день. Он недалеко отсюда*.**
	[Dó-bri dyeny. On nye-da-lye-kó at-syóo-da]
MAN	**А как до него добраться?****
	[A kak da-nye-vó da-brá-tsa?]
WOMAN	**Вам лучше сесть на троллейбус номер один.*****
	[Vam lóo-che syesty na tra-lyéy-boos nó-myer a-deén]
MAN	**Большое спасибо.**
WOMAN	**Пожалуйста.**

*He (=It) is not far from here.
**And how do I get to it?
***It would be best to take trolleybus no. 1.

7 You can't reach the ticket punch

PASSENGER 1	**Передайте, пожалуйста, талон.**
	[Pye-rye-dáy-tye, pa-zhál-sta, ta-lón]
PASSENGER 2	**Хорошо.** [Ha-ra-shó]

8 The Hermitage is the next stop

VISITOR **Эрмита́ж – когда́ выходи́ть?**
[Er-mee-tásh – kag-dá vi-ha-dée'ty?]

PASSENGER **На сле́дующей.***
[Na slyé-doo-yoo-shshyey]

VISITOR **Спаси́бо.**

PASSENGER **Не́ за что́.****
[Nyé za shtó]

*At the next (stop).
**You're welcome (= пожа́луйста).

9 Are you getting off?

PASSENGER 1 **Извини́те*, вы выхо́дите на сле́дующей остано́вке[5]?**
[Eez-vee-née-tye, vi vi-hó-dee-tye na slyé-doo-yoo-shshyey a-sta-nóf-kye?]

PASSENGER 2 **Нет.**

*Excuse me (= Прости́те)

10 Are you getting off?

WOMAN **Вы выхо́дите на сле́дующей остано́вке?**

MAN **Да, выхожу́.**
[Da, vi-ha-zhoó]

DRIVER (announcing the next stop) **Садо́вая у́лица* – сле́дующая остано́вка.**
[Sa-dó-va-ya oó-lee-tsa – slyé-doo-yoo-shsha-ya a-sta-nóf-ka]

*Sadovaya Street crosses Nevsky Prospekt, St Petersburg's main avenue.

11 A friendly taxi driver

PASSENGER **Здра́вствуйте.**

TAXI DRIVER **Здра́вствуйте.**

PASSENGER **Мне на́до в Марии́нский теа́тр.***
[Mnye ná-da vMa-ree-ée'en-skee tye-átr]

TAXI DRIVER **Пожа́луйста, сади́тесь.****
[Pa-zhál-sta, sa-dée-tyesy]

PASSENGER **Спаси́бо.**

*I have to go to the Mariinskii Theatre (St Petersburg's equivalent of Moscow's Bolshoi Theatre).
**Fine, get in.

Word list

автобус (m) [af-tó-boos] — bus
в [v] or [f] — in/to
выходить [vi-ha-dée´ty] — to get out
(я) выхожу [vi-ha-zhoó] — (I) am getting out
до [da] — as far as/until
добраться [da-brá-tsa] — to reach/get to
здесь [zdyesy] — here
как [kak] — how
когда [kag-dá] — when
лучше [loó-che] — better
метро (n) [mye-tró] — metro/underground
мне надо [mnye ná-da] — I have to
музей (m) [moo-zyéy] — museum
на [na] — on/to
надо [ná-da] — it is necessary/one must
номер (m) [nó-myer] — number
он [ón] — he/it (if noun is masculine)
остановка (f) [a-sta-nóf-ka] — stop
отсюда [at-syoó-da] — from here
площадь (f) [pló-shshyaty] — square
передайте [pye-rye-dáy-tye] — pass (it) along
проспект (m) [pra-spyékt] — avenue
садитесь [sa-dée-tyesy] — get in/sit down
сесть [syesty] — to get on (a bus etc.)/to sit down
такси (n) [tak-seé] — taxi
талон (m) [ta-lón] — travel coupon/ticket
театр (m) [tye-átr] — theatre
трамвай (m) [tram-váy] — tram
троллейбус (m) [tra-lyéy-boos] — trolleybus
улица (f) [oó-lee-tsa] — street
Эрмитаж (m) [Er-mee-tásh] — the Hermitage

Explanations

1 Excuse me, can you tell me...?

Begin your request for information with **Прости́те, пожа́луйста** ('Excuse me please') or **Скажи́те, пожа́луйста** ('Tell me please').

Скажи́те, пожа́луйста, где метро́? Could you tell me where the metro is, please?

2 Asking where something is

The key word is **где** [gdye] 'where'. If you find [gdye] hard to say, miss out the [g] and say [dye]. Then add the name of the place.

Где Кра́сная пло́щадь? Where is Red Square?
[Gdye Krá-sna-ya pló-shshyaty?]
Remember there is no equivalent of 'is' in Russian.

Где метро́? Where is the metro?
Где музе́й? Where is the museum?

3 How do I get there?

'How' is **как** [kak]. If you want to walk, you ask **Как пройти́...?** (literally 'How to walk through...?'). If you want to use transport, you ask **Как прое́хать...?** (How to travel through...?). 'There' (in the sense of 'to that place') is **туда́** [too-dá].

Эрмита́ж, пожа́луйста. Как прое́хать туда́? The Hermitage, please. How do I get there (by transport)?

4 (How do I get) to the Russian Museum?

'To' is **в** ('into') with buildings, **на** ('onto') with streets and squares.

Как пройти́ в Ру́сский музе́й? How do I get (on foot) to the Russian Museum?
Как прое́хать в Эрмита́ж? How do I get (by transport) to the Hermitage?

After **в** 'into' and **на** 'onto', masculine and neuter words keep the same form as in the wordlists.

However, feminine nouns ending in **-a** (e.g. **у́лица** 'street') change their ending to **-y** (**у́лицу**). The ending **-y** is the accusative case, an ending we met in Unit 3.

Как прое́хать на у́лицу Пу́шкина? How do I get (by transport) to Pushkin Street (Street of Pushkin)?
Как пройти́ в рестора́н Ара́гви? How do I get (on foot) to the Aragvi Restaurant?

5 Are you getting off?

You need the question **Вы выхо́дите?** [Vi vi-hó-dee-tye?] when you want to get off a bus or tram. Public transport is often very crowded. You push your way on at the back (look for **вход** [fhot] 'entrance'). To get to the exit doors (**вы́ход** [ví-hat] 'exit'), which are at the front, you may have to squeeze past a lot of large Russians. To give yourself enough time, start making for the exit well in advance. But instead of just pushing, ask the person blocking your path **Вы выхо́дите** [Vi vi-hó-dee-tye?] If the answer is **нет** [nyet], he/she will try to get out of your way. If it's **да** [da], just follow along behind while he/she does the asking.

Exercises

1 Give English equivalents for
(a) напра́во
(b) нале́во
(c) пря́мо
(d) На́до прое́хать три остано́вки.

2 Play the part of the visitor

VISITOR	(Excuse me, where is the metro?)
RUSSIAN	На́до сесть на тролле́йбус но́мер шесть и прое́хать две остано́вки.
VISITOR	(Where is the stop?)
RUSSIAN	Вот напра́во.
VISITOR	(Thank you)
RUSSIAN	Пожа́луйста.

3 Ask:

(a) where the Russia Hotel (гости́ница Росси́я) is.

(b) where the metro is.

(c) how to get to the Bolshoi Theatre (Большо́й теа́тр) on foot.

(d) how to get there by transport.

4 Fill in your part of the conversation and translate the answer

YOU (Could you tell me where Red Square is, please?)

RUSSIAN Кра́сная пло́щадь за угло́м и пря́мо по у́лице.

5 RUSSIAN Вы выхо́дите?

  YOU (No)

What should you now do?

6 Fill in your part of the conversation (You won't recognise all the grammatical endings, but try to understand the meaning.)

YOU (Excuse me, where is the Hermitage?)

RUSSIAN Э́то далеко́. В нача́ле Не́вского проспе́кта.

YOU (Excuse me, I don't understand. Please would you repeat?)

RUSSIAN На Не́вском проспе́кте. Не́вский проспе́кт.

YOU (And how do I get there by transport?)

RUSSIAN Вам лу́чше сесть на тролле́йбус но́мер два́дцать два.

YOU (Repeat, please)

RUSSIAN Тролле́йбус но́мер два́дцать два.

YOU (Thank you)

Worth knowing

Public transport

Many Russian cities, including Moscow and St Petersburg, have a metro **(метро́)** 'underground', and all journeys cost the same, regardless of distance.

There are no tickets. You buy tokens at the entrance, put one in the slot beside the automatic barrier, watch for the white light, and pass through the narrow gap. If you don't put in a token, two metal arms shoot out of the barrier with a crash and attempt to chop you in half.

Moscow metro stations are palatial, with polished marble, chandeliers and sculptures. The authorities, evidently regarding station nameboards as unaesthetic, keep the number of signs giving the name of the station to the minimum; for example, there are almost never any names on the platform side of the tracks. So even if you can read Russian you may find it hard, especially in a crowded carriage, to spot a station name to read. However, the names of the stops are always announced over the train's loudspeaker system. Here is a sample of a metro announcement:

Ста́нция Охо́тный ряд ... Осторо́жно, две́ри закрыва́ются. Сле́дующая ста́нция Лубя́нка.
Okhotny Ryad ('Hunters' Row') Station. Careful, the doors are closing. The next station is Lubyanka.

Buses, trams and trolleybuses are also one price, but you need a ticket. Conductors are rare and most cities now require you to buy a book of tickets from a kiosk; you can also get them from the driver. <u>You must then validate one of these tickets using one of the metal punches (компóстер) screwed to the wall of the bus.</u> If you can't reach a punch because of the crush, ask the person you're squeezed against to pass your ticket along to somebody who can reach. Say **Передáйте, пожáлуйста** ('Pass it along, please'). If you want to keep busy during a journey, stand beside a ticket punch on a crowded bus. If you travel without a valid ticket, you may be fined by an inspector **(контролёр),** usually a harmless-looking old woman disguised in peasant clothes who suddenly reveals an official identity card and a ferocious manner.

To buy tickets in the bus say to the driver: **Кнúжку** [Kneésh-koo], **пожáлуйста.** He will sell you a **кнúжка** (booklet) of ten tickets.

Taxis
A taxi driver may refuse to take you if he doesn't like your choice of direction. If you don't feel like a long argument, you may find an offer to pay in dollars very persuasive.

When taxis are in short supply, do what the Russians do: flag down any passing private motorist and agree a price for the journey.

5 Times and days

Key expressions

When does the museum open?	**Когда музей открывается?** [Kag-dá moo-zyéy at-kri-vá-ye-tsa?]
When does it close?	**Когда он закрывается?** [za-kri-vá-ye-tsa]
(at) one o'clock	**(в) час** [(f) chas]
(at) two o'clock	**(в) два часа** [(v) dva chee-sá]
(at) five o'clock	**(в) пять часов** [(v) pyaty chee-sóf]
this evening	**сегодня вечером** [sye-vód-nya vyé-chye-ram] (Note: here г is pronounced as [v])
May I speak to Nina?	**Позовите, пожалуйста, Нину** [Pa-za-veé-tye, pa-zhál-sta, Neé-noo]
Don't hang up	**Не кладите трубку** [Nye kla-deé-tye troóp-koo]
Speak slowly, please	**Говорите медленно, пожалуйста.** [Ga-va-reé-tye myé-dlye-na, pa-zhál-sta]
Do you speak English?	**Вы говорите по-английски?** [Vi ga-va-reé-tye pa-an-gleé-skee?]
That's agreed/OK	**Договорились** [Da-ga-va-reé-leesy]

| I'm sorry, it was accidental | **Прости́те, я неча́янно.** [Pra-steé-tye, ya nye-chá-ya-na] |
| It doesn't matter | **Ничего́** [Nee-chye-vó] (Note: here г is pronounced as [v]) |

Conversations

1 When does the museum open?

TOURIST **Когда́ музе́й открыва́ется?**
[Kag-dá moo-zyéy at-kri-vá-ye-tsa?]

GUIDE **В де́сять часо́в[1].**
[Vdyé-syaty chee-sóf]

2 When does it close?

TOURIST **Когда́ он[2] закрыва́ется?**
[Kag-dá ón za-kri-vá-ye-tsa?]

GUIDE **В шесть[1].**
[Fshesty]

3 Is it open every day?

TOURIST **Музе́й рабо́тает ка́ждый день?**
[Moo-zyéy ra-bó-ta-yet kázh-di dyeny?]

GUIDE **Ка́ждый день кро́ме понеде́льника.***
[Kázh-di dyeny kró-mye pa-nye-dyély-nee-ka]

*Every day except Monday.

4 You want to be woken in the morning

GUEST **До́брый ве́чер. Мо́жно[3] меня́ разбуди́ть за́втра в семь часо́в утра́[4]?***
[Dó-bri vyé-chyer. Mózh-na mye-nyá raz-boo-deéty záf-tra fsyemy chee-sóf oo-trá?]

MAID **Да, коне́чно, в семь утра́ я вас разбужу́.*** [Da, ka-nyésh-na, fsyemy oo-trá ya vas raz-boo-zhoó]

*Can you wake me tomorrow at 7 am?

**Yes, of course, at 7am I'll wake you. (Note: ч in 'коне́чно' pronounced as [sh])

5 Ordering a taxi

GUEST **Мо́жно[3] заказа́ть такси́?**

	[Mózh-na za-ka-záty tak-seé?]
ASSISTANT	**Какóе врéмя?***
	[Ka-kó-ye vryé-mya?]
GUEST	**Сегóдня вéчером.**
	[Sye-vód-nya vyé-chye-ram]
ASSISTANT	**Тóчное врéмя?****
	[Tóch-na-ye vryé-mya?]
GUEST	**Семь часóв вéчера[4].**
	[Syemy chee-sóf vyé-chye-ra]
ASSISTANT	**Кудá поéдете?*****
	[Koo-dá pa-yé-dye-tye?]
GUEST	**В Большóй теáтр.**
	[VBaly-shóy tye-átr]
ASSISTANT	**Так, стóимость закáза – два дóллара.*******
	[Tak, stó-ee-masty za-ká-za – dva dó-la-ra]
GUEST	**Хорошó.**

*What time?

**The exact time?

***Where will you be going?

****Right, the order costs two dollars.

6 Arranging a meeting

WOMAN	**Приходúте к нам в понедéльник[5].***
	[Pree-ha-deé-tye knam fpa-nye-dyély-neek]
MAN	**В понедéльник я зáнят. Я могý в срéду úли в пя́тницу[5].****
	[Fpa-nye-dyély-neek ya zá-nyat. Ya ma-goó eé-lee fsryé-doo eé-lee fpyát-nee-tsoo]
WOMAN	**Хорошó. Тогдá приходúте[6] в пя́тницу.**
	[Ha-ra-shó. Tag-dá pree-ha-deé-tye fpyát-nee-tsoo]
	Договорúлись.
	[Da-ga-va-reé-leesy]
MAN	**Договорúлись.**

*Come and see us on Monday.

**On Monday I'm busy. I can come either on Wednesday or on Friday.

7 Taking down a phone number

MAN 1 **Скажи́те, пожа́луйста, ваш телефо́н.**
[Ska-zhí-tye, pa-zhál-sta, vash tye-lye-fón]

MAN 2 **Пять·во́семь·шесть два·оди́н три·де́вять.**

MAN 1 **Повтори́те, пожа́луйста.**

MAN 2 **Хорошо́. 5 8 6 2 1 3 9.**

8 Please give that number slowly

MAN **Скажи́те, пожа́луйста, телефо́н Ка́ти*.**
[Ska-zhí-tye, pa-zhál-sta, tye-lye-fón Ká-tee]

WOMAN **Две́сти девяно́сто - со́рок - со́рок четы́ре**

MAN **Пожа́луйста, говори́те ме́дленно. Я иностра́нец.**

WOMAN **Ой, извини́те, пожа́луйста. 290 40 44.**

*Please tell me Katya's telephone number.

9 Ivan Ivanovich isn't in? I'll ring back.

CLERK **Алле́!**
[A-lyó!]

CALLER **Здра́вствуйте, позови́те, пожа́луйста, Ива́на Ива́новича[7].**

CLERK **Его́ нет.***
[Ye-vó nyet]

CALLER **А когда́ он бу́дет?**

CLERK **Он бу́дет че́рез час.****

CALLER **Спаси́бо. Я перезвоню́.**

CLERK **Пожа́луйста.**

*He's out. (Note: г in 'его' is pronounced as [v])
**He'll be here in an hour.

10 Ivan Petrovich isn't back. When will he come?

CLERK **Слу́шаю.**

CALLER **Здра́вствуйте. Позови́те, пожа́луйста, Ива́на Петро́вича[7].**
[Pa-za-veé-tye, pa-zhál-sta, Ee-vá-na Pye-tró-vee-cha]

CLERK **Его́ сего́дня не бу́дет.***
[Ye-vó sye-vód-nya nye boo-dyet]

CALLER **Не клади́те, пожа́луйста, тру́бку. А когда́ он придёт?****
[Nye kla-deé-tye, pa-zhál-sta, troóp-koo. A kag-dá ón pree-dyót?]

CLERK **Óн бýдет тóлько зáвтра. *****
[Ón boo-dyet tóly-ka záf-tra]
CALLER **Спасúбо.**
CLERK **До свидáния.**

*He won't be here today.
**And when will he come?
***He won't be here until tomorrow.

11 Apologising

MAN **Óй!** [Óy!] (Exclamation)
GIRL **Простúте, пожáлуйста, я нечáянно.**
[Pra-stée-tye, pa-zhál-sta, ya nye-chá-ya-na]
MAN **Ничегó, ничегó. Пожáлуйста.**
[Nee-chye-<u>v</u>ó, nee-chye-<u>v</u>ó]

Word list

аллё [a-lyó]	hello (on phone)
(óн) бýдет	(he) will be
ваш	your
вéчером [vyé-chye-ram]	in the evening
врéмя (n) [vryé-mya]	time
дáйте [dáy-tye]	give
двéсти [dvyé-stee]	two hundred
день (m) [dyeny]	day
зáвтра [záf-tra]	tomorrow
(я) зáнят [ya zá-nyat]	(I'm) busy (man)
(я) занятá [ya za-nee-tá]	(I'm) busy (woman)
заказáть [za-ka-záty]	to order
(музéй) закрывáется [za-kri-vá-ye-tsa]	(the museum) closes
úли	either/or
(я) иностáнец (m) [ya ee-na-strá-nyets]	(I'm) a foreigner (man)
(я) инострáнка (f) [ya ee-na-strán-ka]	(I'm) a foreigner (woman)
кáждый [kázh-di]	every
конéчно [ka-nyé<u>sh</u>-na]	of course

кро́ме [kró-mye]	except
куда́ [koo-dá]	(to) where
меня́ [mye-nyá]	me
(я) могу́ [ya ma-goó]	(I) can
ноль [nóly]	zero
(музей) открыва́ется	(the museum) opens
(я) перезвоню́	(I)'ll ring back
[ya pye-rye-zva-nyoó]	
позови́те	call
приходи́те к нам	come and see us
[pree-ha-dée-tye]	(come to us)
(музе́й) рабо́тает	(the museum) works (i.e. is open)
разбуди́ть	to wake
[raz-boo-déety]	
сего́дня	today
[sye-vód-nya]	
такси́ (n) [tak-sée]	taxi
телефо́н (m)	telephone/phone number
че́рез час	in an hour
[chyé-ryes chas]	

Explanations

1 Telling the time

The word for 'hour' is **час** [chas], which also means 'o'clock' and 'one o'clock'. After 2, 3 and 4, **час** has the ending **-а**; after 5, 6 etc. the ending is **-ов**:

час	one o'clock/one hour
два часа́ [dva chee-sá]	two o'clock/two hours
три часа́	three o'clock/three hours
семь часо́в	seven o'clock/hours
[syemy chee-sóf]	
де́сять часо́в	ten o'clock/hours

'Minute' is **мину́та** [mee-noó-ta]. After 2, 3 and 4 it becomes **мину́ты** and after 5, 6 etc. **мину́т**:

одна́ мину́та	one minute
две мину́ты	two minutes
де́сять мину́т	ten minutes
три́дцать мину́т	thirty minutes

If you put these two constructions together, you can give any time using the 24-hour clock.

Пятна́дцать часо́в де́сять мину́т: 15.10
This is what you will hear in loudspeaker announcements or on the radio.

To say 'at a time' simply put **в** ('in', 'at') in front of the time:
в два часа́ at two o'clock

Other useful time phrases:

What time is it?	**Кото́рый час?** [Ka-tó-ri chas?] ('which hour?')
yesterday	**вчера́** [fchye-rá]
in the morning	**у́тром** [óo-tram]

2   He/she/it

All Russian nouns are masculine, feminine or neuter (see page 29). So even when you're talking about *things* rather than about people, you say 'he' (rather than 'it') for masculine nouns and 'she' for feminine nouns.

Музе́й is masculine, so 'it closes' is **он закрыва́ется** ('he'). 'She' (used for feminine nouns such as **у́лица** 'street') is **она́** [a-ná].

'It' is **оно́** [a-nó]. This word is used for neuter nouns, but is not very common.

3   Is it possible?/May I?/Can you?

Мо́жно [mózh-na] covers all three of these. Just find in your dictionary the verb which describes what you want to do, or what you want somebody else to do, and put it after **мо́жно.**

Мо́жно войти́? [Mózh-na vay-tée?] May I come in? (Is it possible to enter?)

Мо́жно меня́ разбуди́ть? [Mózh-na mye-nyá raz-boo-dée ty?] Can you wake me? (Is it possible me to wake?)

Мо́жно закури́ть? [Mózh-na za-koo-reéty?] Is it possible to start smoking? (May I smoke?)

Мо́жно заказа́ть такси́? [Mózh-na za-ka-záty tak-seé?] Is it possible to order a taxi?

'You may' is simply **мо́жно.**
'It's not possible' is **нельзя́** [nyely-zyá].

4 am/pm

To say am or pm, the Russians use the following four words:
утра́ [oo-trá] ('of the morning') 4am to midday
дня [dnya] ('of the day') midday to 5 or 6pm
ве́чера [vyé-chye-ra] ('of the evening') 5 or 6 pm
  to midnight
но́чи [nó-chee] ('of the night') midnight to 4am
в семь часо́в ве́чера at 7pm

5 Days of the week (abbreviations in brackets)

Monday	**понеде́льник (пн)** [pa-nye-dyély-neek] по=after+не=not+дел=do-day 'the day after the day you rest'	
Tuesday	**вто́рник (вт)** [ftór-neek] 'second day'	
Wednesday	**среда́ (ср)** [srye-dá] 'middle day'	
Thursday	**четве́рг (чт)** [chyet-vyérk] 'fourth day'	
Friday	**пя́тница (пт)** [pyát-nee-tsa] 'fifth day'	
Saturday	**суббо́та (сб)** [soo-bó-ta] 'Sabbath'	
Sunday	**воскресе́нье (вс)** [vas-krye-syé-nyye] 'resurrection'	

To say *on* a particular day, simply use **в** again. With **в**, the three feminine nouns – i.e. the words ending in **-а** – change the ending to **-у**. The words for the other four days, which are masculine **(понеде́льник, вто́рник, четве́рг)** or neuter **(воскресе́нье),** stay the same.

6 Giving instructions

The ordering form (the 'imperative') of most verbs ends **-айте** [-ay-tye] or **-ите** [-ee-tye]. You know examples such as:

Говори́те ме́дленно	Speak slowly
Скажи́те	Tell (me)

To sound polite, just add the word **пожа́луйста**.

Да́йте, пожа́луйста, ко́фе	Please give me a coffee
Напиши́те э́то, пожа́луйста	Write it down, please
Позови́те, пожа́луйста, Ната́шу	Please call Natasha

7 Please call Natasha

Позови́те Ната́шу. Ната́шу is the accusative case of **Ната́ша** after **позови́те** 'call' (see page 43). All names which end in **-а** change to **-у**. And so **Ната́ша** becomes **Ната́шу.** Names of people which end in a consonant, like **Ива́н** or **Влади́мир**, *add* **-а**: so 'Call Ivan Ivanovich' is: **Позови́те Ива́на Ива́новича** [Pa-za-vee-tye Ee-va-na Ee-va-na-vee-cha].

Exercises

1 Translate into English

(a) Два часа́.
(b) Два́дцать два часа́.
(c) Шесть часо́в три́дцать мину́т.
(d) Музе́й открыва́ется в оди́ннадцать часо́в.
(e) Рестора́н закрыва́ется в двена́дцать часо́в.
(f) В сре́ду.
(g) Приходи́те в пя́тницу и́ли в суббо́ту.
(h) Приходи́те в четве́рг ве́чером.

2 What is the time according to Moscow Radio?

(Моско́вское вре́мя 'Moscow Time')
(a) Моско́вское вре́мя – трина́дцать часо́в.
(b) Моско́вское вре́мя – двена́дцать часо́в одна́ мину́та.

3 Say 'I'll come' (**Я приду́** [Ya pree-doo])

(a) on Saturday
(b) at three o'clock
(c) in the evening
(d) tomorrow
(e) tomorrow evening

4 What are the working hours of this office?

пн, ср, пт 9-13
вт, чт, сб 14-18

5 Write down the following telephone numbers

(If you have the cassette, try and work out the
numbers without looking at the words)

(a) Двести пятьдесят шесть – ноль два –
тридцать пять

(b) Сто двадцать пять – семьдесят – девяносто
девять

6 Play the part of the foreigner

FOREIGNER   (Excuse me, when does the museum
               open?)
RECEPTIONIST   В десять.
FOREIGNER   (Repeat please)
RECEPTIONIST   Он открывается в десять часов.
FOREIGNER   (And when does it close?)
RECEPTIONIST   В восемь часов вечера.
FOREIGNER   (Thank you)

7 Order a taxi

YOU   (Hello. Can I order a taxi?)
CLERK   Можно. Когда?
YOU   (This evening)
CLERK   Точное время?
YOU   (Eight o'clock)
CLERK   Куда поедете?
YOU   (To the restaurant Uzbekistan)
CLERK   Хорошо. С вас два доллара за заказ.

8 Make a phone call

WOMAN   Да.
YOU   (Can I speak to Natasha, please?)
WOMAN   Её сейчас нет.
YOU   (Speak slowly, please. I'm a foreigner.)
WOMAN   Её нет. Она придёт часов в восемь.
YOU   (Please repeat.)
WOMAN   Она придёт в восемь часов.
YOU   (OK, I'll ring back at eight.)

Worth Knowing

Public buildings such as shops, cafés and museums exhibit notices with their opening hours in figures – but be warned that all of these, including shops, are unlikely to admit customers up to half an hour *before* closing time.

МУЗЕЙ РАБОТАЕТ

Пн	10·00ч –	17·00ч
Вт	—	—
Ср	10·00ч –	17·00ч
Чт	10·00ч –	17·00ч
Пт	10·00ч –	17·00ч
Сб	10·00ч –	17·00ч
Вс	10·00ч –	17·00ч

Timetables

Russian timetables use the twenty-four hour clock. But note one curious aspect of transport in Moscow-centric Russia: despite the twelve time-zones, all transport timetables use Moscow time (**Моско́вское вре́мя**), and so do all airport and station clocks. So you might fly into Irkutsk in Eastern Siberia at 5 pm according to the timetable and all the clocks, but outside it's pitch dark. Locally it's 11 pm – and if you find the restaurant closed, that's because it works on local time.

Telephoning

Most Russian flats have a phone (**телефóн**), and there are plenty of public call boxes (**автомáт**), from which a call currently costs fifteen kopecks. In addition, your hotel room will almost certainly contain a direct line telephone and you will not be charged for local calls. People you meet will willingly give you their phone numbers, so it is worth learning the basic phrases for making contact by phone.

Russians use telephones all the time but they tend to be abrupt. When answering a call, they say **Да!** or **Слýшаю!** ('I'm listening'), never anything informative such as their name or number. When you ring an office number you are likely to find that if the person you want isn't there, or your request isn't immediately understood, the phone is banged down without even **До свидáния.** So learn the phrase **Не кладúте трýбку, пожáлуйста!** [Nye kla-dée-tye tro͞op-koo, pa-zhál-sta] 'Don't hang up' – and learn to say it quickly.

6 Socialising

Key expressions

What's your name?	**Как вас зову́т?** [Kak vas za-vo´ot?]
My name is...	**Меня́ зову́т...** [Mye-nyá za-vo´ot...]
Pleased to meet you	**О́чень прия́тно** [Ó-chyeny pree-yát-na]
Your health!	**Ва́ше здоро́вье!** [Váshe zda-ró-vyye!]
I like Moscow.	**Мне нра́вится Москва́** [Mnye nrá-vee-tsa Mask-vá]
I don't like...	**Мне не нра́вится...** [Mnye nye nrá-vee-tsa]
It's very tasty	**О́чень вку́сно** [Ó-chyeny fko´o-sna]
I can't eat any more	**Я сыт** [Ya sit] (man) **Я сыта́** [si-tá] (woman)
I am (not) married	**Я (не) за́мужем** (woman) [Ya (nye) zá-moo-zhem] **Я (не) жена́т** (man) [Ya (nye) zhe-nát]

You will hear:

Познако́мьтесь [Pa-zna-kómy-tyesy]	Let me introduce you
Бери́те [Bye-re´e-tye]	Do take some
Нали́ть ещё? [Na-le´ety ye-shshyó?]	Can I pour you some more?
Ми́лости про́сим [Me´e-la-stee pró-seem]	Welcome
Раздева́йтесь [Raz-dye-váy-tyesy]	Take your coat and shoes off (lit. 'Undress')

Conversations

1 Finding out names

GIRL **Скажи́те, как вас зову́т?**
[Ska-zhí-tye, kak vas za-vo'ot?]

BOY **Меня́ зову́т Вита́лий. А как вас зову́т?**
[Mye-nyá za-vo'ot Vee-tá-lee. A kak vas za-vo'ot?]

GIRL **Меня́ зову́т Мари́я.** [Ma-ree-ya]

2 Asking someone's name

LITTLE GIRL **Скажи́те, пожа́луйста, как вас зову́т?** [Ska-zhí-tye, pa-zhál-sta, kak vas za-vo'ot?]

WOMAN **Меня́ зову́т Ири́на Влади́мировна[1].**
[Mye-nyá za-vo'ot Ee-ree-na Vla-dee-mee-rav-na]

3 What are your first name and patronymic?

GIRL **Скажи́те, как ва́ше и́мя и о́тчество[1]?**
[kak vá-she ee-mya ee ó-chye-stva?]

BOY **Вита́лий Григо́рьевич. А как ва́ше и́мя и о́тчество?**

GIRL **Мари́я Арка́дьевна.** [Ar-ká-dyyev-na]

4 Formal introductions

MAN 1 **Меня́ зову́т Алексе́й Эдуа́рдович.**
[A-lyek-syéy E-doo-ár-da-veech]

MAN 2 **О́чень прия́тно.**

MAN 1 **А как зову́т вас?**

MAN 2 **Меня́ зову́т Алекса́ндр Миха́йлович.**
[A-lyek-sándr Mee-háy-la-veech]

MAN 1 **О́чень прия́тно.**

5 Introducing people by first names

MAN **Здра́вствуйте, дороги́е, э́то во́т мо́й брат Семён.* Познако́мьтесь. Э́то Ко́ля.**

SEMYON **О́чень прия́тно.**

MAN **Э́то Фили́ппа.**

*Hello, my friends ('dears'), this is (here) my brother Semyon.

SEMYON	Óчень прия́тно.
MAN	Это Ле́на.
SEMYON	Óчень прия́тно.
MAN	Га́ля.

6 Guests arrive

EVERYBODY	Здра́вствуйте!
HOSTESS	Проходи́те. Проходи́те. Раздева́йтесь. Вот та́почки.
GUESTS	Спаси́бо. Спаси́бо.
HOSTESS	Ми́лости про́сим.

7 Toasts

Мир и сча́стье.* [Meer ee shshá-styye]
Дава́йте вы́пьем за знако́мство[2].**
[Da-váy-tye ví-pyyem za zna-kóm-stva]
Дава́йте вы́пьем за дру́жбу и мир на земле́.***
[za dróozh-boo ee meer na zyem-lyé]

*Peace and happiness.

**Let's drink to our meeting.

***Let's drink to friendship and peace on earth.

8 Very tasty

GUEST	Óчень вку́сно! Óчень вку́сно! Про́сто замеча́тельно! [Pró-sta za-mye-chá-tely-na!]
HOSTESS	Ку́шай на здоро́вье.* [Kóo-shay na zda-ró-vyye]
GUEST	Спаси́бо. Óчень вку́сно.

*'Eat to your health', a polite reply to praise of food

9 Taking down an address

MAN	Скажи́те, пожа́луйста, где вы[3] живёте?
WOMAN	На Арба́те*: Арба́т, дом пятна́дцать, кварти́ра семь[4].
MAN	Арба́т, дом 15, кварти́ра 7.

*On the Arbat, a historic street in central Moscow.

10 A new friend gives her number

GIRL 1   **Мой телефон сто шестьдесят восемь - пятьдесят четыре - одиннадцать.**

GIRL 2   **Повтори[3], пожалуйста, я запишу.***

GIRL 1   **168 54 11. Позвони[3] вечером, пожалуйста.**

GIRL 2   **Хорошо.**

GIRL 1   **До свидания.**

GIRL 2   **Пока.**** [Pa-ká.]

*I'll write (it) down.

**See you (colloquial goodbye).

11 Taking a phone number

GIRL 1   **Мой телефон - сто пятьдесят один - ноль шесть - ноль два.**

GIRL 2   **Хорошо. Я обязательно позвоню.***

*I'll definitely phone.

12 Arranging to telephone

GIRL 1   **Позвоните завтра вечером.**

GIRL 2   **А когда?**

GIRL 1   **В девять часов.**

GIRL 2   **Хорошо.**

13 Do you like St Petersburg?

GIRL 1   **Вам нравится Пегербург[5]?**

GIRL 2   **Конечно, очень нравится.**

14 Do you like Moscow?

ADULT   **Тебе нравится[5] Москва?**

CHILD   **Да, очень.**

15 Taking leave

GUEST   **Спасибо вам большое, было очень приятно.***

HOSTESS   **Спасибо вам.**

GUEST   **К сожалению, нам пора уходить.** До завтра.***** [Ksa-zha-lyé-nee-yoo]

HOSTESS   **До свидания.**

*it was very nice.

**Unfortunately, it's time for us to leave.

***See you tomorrow (Until tomorrow).

Word list

а́дрес (m)	address
брат (m)	brother
бы́ло	(it) was
ва́ше и́мя (n) [e'e-mya]	your first name
го́род (m) [gó-rat]	city/town
дава́йте вы́пьем	let's drink
до за́втра [da záf-tra]	see you tomorrow
до́м (m)	house/building
дру́жба (f)	friendship
(вы) живёте	(you) live
[vi zhi-vyó-tye]	
замеча́тельно	marvellous
кварти́ра (f)	flat
мир (m)	peace
мир на земле́	peace on earth
мо́й	my
обяза́тельно	definitely
[a-bee-zá-tyely-na]	
о́тчество (n)	patronymic
[ó-chye-stva]	
позвони́те	ring (me)
(я) позвоню́	(I'll) phone
пока́ [pa-ká]	see you soon
прия́тно	pleasant
про́сто	simply
проходи́те	come through
[pra-ha-de'e-tye]	
сча́стье (n) [shshá-styye]	happiness
та́почки (f) [tá-pach-kee]	slippers (nobody wears outdoor shoes at home, and there are always spare pairs for guests)
фами́лия (f) [fa-me'e-lee-ya]	surname

Family relationships

ба́бушка (f) [bá-boosh-ka]	grandmother

брат (m) [brat]   brother
дéдушка (m – despite the -a)   grandfather
    [dyé-doosh-ka]
дóчь (f) [dóchy]   daughter
женá (f) [zhe-ná]   wife
муж (m) [moosh]   husband
сестрá (f) [sye-strá]   sister
сын (m) [sin]   son

Explanations

1 Names

Every Russian has three names. The first name
(**ймя**) [ée-mya] is a given name, like ours: **Натáлья**
[Na-tá-lyya], **Влади́мир** [Vla-dée-meer], **Ивáн**
[Ee-ván], **Татья́на** [Ta-tyyá-na], **Михаи́л** [Mee-ha-éel]
etc. These first names all have 'intimate' forms,
used by friends and family: **Натáша** [Na-tá-sha]
from **Натáлья**, **Волóдя** [Va-ló-dya] from **Влади́мир**,
Вáня [Vá-nya] from **Ивáн**, **Тáня** [Tá-nya] from
Татья́на etc.

The last name is a surname: **Горбачёв** [Gar-ba-
chyóf], **Карéнин** [Ka-ryé-neen]. These surnames
are male forms; women add a feminine ending:
Горбачёва [Gar-ba-chyó-va], **Карéнина** [Ka-ryé-
nee-na].

The middle name is formed from the father's first
name and is called a patronymic (**óтчество**); men
add **-ович** [o-veech/a-veech] to their father's first
name: **Ивáнович** [Ee-vá-na-veech], **Влади́мирович**
[Vla-dée-mee-ra-veech], while women add **-овна**
[ov-na/av-na]: **Ивáновна** [Ee-vá-nav-na],
Влади́мировна [Vla-dée-mee-rav-na], **Михáйловна**
[Mee-háy-lav-na] etc.

Foreigners should know about patronymics for one
important reason: when you speak to someone to
whom you want to be polite, **Михаи́л Сергéевич
Горбачёв** [Mee-ha-éel Syer-gyé-ye-veech Gar-ba-
chyóf], for example, you use *his first name and*

patronymic, and call him **Михаи́л Серге́евич**
[Mee-ha-e'el Syer-gyé-ye-veech], which is the
equivalent of calling him 'Mr Gorbachev' in
English. Russian has no generally used equivalent
of Mr/Mrs/Miss/Ms. Even **това́рищ** [ta-vá-reeshsh]
'comrade' is relatively rare and should not be used
by foreigners. Learning these double names is hard
work to begin with, but your politeness and effort
will be appreciated. Try to find out the first name
and patronymic of anyone you will have repeated
dealings with.

2 Toasts

During alcoholic social occasions, Russians like to
begin each round with a different toast (almost the
same word in Russian: **то́ст**). The toasts tend to
get more and more elaborate as the evening
progresses. You will be expected to propose toasts
too, so here is a list of simpler ones. Each one
starts with the word **за** [za] which literally means
'for'.

Вы́пьем...	Let's drink...
за мир	to peace
за дру́жбу	to friendship
за вас	to you
за на́шу дру́жбу	to our friendship
за а́нгло-ру́сскую дру́жбу	to Anglo-Russian friendship
за же́нщин	to women

3 You: вы (polite) and ты (familiar)

People you don't know well are addressed as **вы**
[vi] ('you') and so is any group of more than one
person. To someone you call **вы** you say

Здра́вствуйте [Zdrá-stvooy-<u>tye</u>]	Hello
Прости́те [Pra-ste'e-tye]	Excuse me
Повтори́те [Pa-fta-re'e-tye]	Repeat

A friend, a relative or a child is addressed as **ты** [ti]
(like 'tu' in French). The words above lose their **-те**
when you speak to someone you call **ты**.

Здра́вствуй [Zdrá-stvooy]   Hello
Прости́ [Pra-steé]   Excuse me
Повтори́ [Pa-fta-reé]   Repeat

4   Russian addresses

Most Russians live in flats, though in the outskirts and in the countryside you will still find the traditional one-family wooden houses with carved windows. A block of flats is a **дóм** [dóm], a word which can also mean 'house' or any building, whether it contains flats or offices or shops. Each **дóм** has a number, but take note that the same number may cover several buildings, usually one behind the other; each of these same-numbered buildings is called a **кóрпус** ('block'). If you are given a private address, it may look like this:

Москва́ (+ six-figure postcode)
у́лица Пу́шкина
дóм 6, кóрпус 2, кварти́ра 153
Ивано́ву Н.Н.

Pushkin Street, building no. 6, block no. 2, flat 153, *to* Mr N.N. Ivanov (with the surname in a form called the dative case). The words **дóм** etc. are often omitted, but the house, block and flat number are always given in that order, i.e. 6/2/153. The city always comes first and the resident's name last.

5   I like the flat

'I like' is **Мне нра́вится** (literally 'To me pleases...'). Just add the word for whatever it is you like: 'flat' is **кварти́ра**. So **Мне нра́вится кварти́ра.**

The question 'Do you like Moscow?' is **Вам нра́вится Москва́?** ('To you pleases Moscow?')

If you're talking to someone you know well – someone you would call **ты** – **вам** changes to **тебе́**:

Тебе́ нра́вится Москва́?

Exercises

1 Say in Russian
(a) My name is ... (fill in your name)
(b) What is your name?

2 What are the names of the people?
(a) Меня зовут Ирина Николаевна.
(b) Меня зовут Татьяна Александровна.

3 Play the part of the foreigner
YOUR FRIEND   Познакомьтесь. Это моя жена Вера.
YOU   (Pleased to meet you)
VERA   Вам нравится Москва?
YOU   (Very much)

4 Play the part of the guest
HOST   Налить вам ещё?
YOU   (Please do *or* No thank you)
HOST   Берите ещё.
YOU   (No thank you, I'm full)
HOST   Берите, берите.
YOU   (Thank you, I can't)

5 To what and whom is this Russian (recorded in a St Petersburg – Moscow sleeper) raising his glass? (народ means 'people')
Мы выпьем за нашу дружбу, мы выпьем за английский народ.

6 Propose one or all of these toasts
YOUR HOST   За что выпьем?
YOU   (To peace/to friendship/to Anglo-Russian friendship/to you/to us/to Natasha)

Worth knowing

Meeting Russians at home
Russians in big cities tend to be short of space (two rooms for a family of three is common) and they may be nervous about inviting you to their rather cramped flats. However, if you make it clear that you would love to visit a Russian home, they

are usually happy to oblige. Socialising at home, often in the kitchen, is very much part of Russian life – there are few pubs, beer bars are often sordid, cafés are scarce, and restaurants, with their loud bands and relatively high prices, are for dancing and drinking rather than talking.

If the invitation is made a day or two in advance, you can expect to be served a full-scale meal in the main room of the flat and the hosts will have spent most of the day preparing it (and who knows how much money on the ingredients). Here you will find good traditional Russian cooking of a kind that is simply not provided in hotels or the main restaurants: various kinds of marinated mushrooms, elaborate salads, rich soup in which you can stand a spoon upright. The whole evening will be spent round the dining table and the meal will not be a rushed affair.

If the invitation is issued on the spot, you will probably sit round the kitchen table and the hosts will bring out everything they happen to have in the flat, which will probably be bread **(хлеб)**, cold sausage **(колбаса́)** and cheese **(сыр)**, perhaps some pickled cabbage **(капу́ста)** or mushrooms (**грибы́**), and tea **(чай).** Russians do not normally keep alcohol at home: it is bought for each occasion, and no bottle is ever left unfinished (most Russian vodka bottles have tear-off tops, and, once opened, they *cannot* be closed). So take a bottle of vodka from your hotel shop. Take other things too (see the presents section opposite). Presents, particularly from foreigners, are very much appreciated.

When you enter, you should take off your shoes. **Та́почки** [tá-pach-kee] 'slippers' will be provided. Then you will be offered the chance to **помы́ть ру́ки** [pa-mítee ró'o-kee] 'wash your hands'. In modern Russian flats, the toilet and bathroom are separate small windowless rooms side by side; the toilet is normally the door on the right.

One of the first things you are likely to be asked is 'Are you married?' The translation of 'married' depends on whether you are a man or a woman. A woman is **замужем** [zá-moo-zhem] (lit. 'behind a husband'); a man is **женáт** [zhe-nát] 'wifed'.

Вы зáмужем?	Are you (a woman) married?
Нет, не зáмужем.	No, I'm not.

Presents for Russians

Giving and receiving presents is an important part of Russian social life. You are likely to make many new friends, since Russians are sociable and hospitable and interested in foreign visitors, so take plenty of small presents. One consequence of the shortages and high prices of many consumer goods is that choosing presents is easy. Go round to your local supermarket and stock up on jars of instant coffee, tins of tea, spices, attractively packaged sweets and savoury snacks. Cosmetics are always welcome, though Russians tend to want famous brands, and so are blank cassettes, clothing (preferably with a visible Western brand name), books in English (modern novels), pocket calculators and video films.

Can you 'Get By'?

Where there are several possible answers give the simplest.

Read and translate these signs

1) РЕСТОРА́Н
2) ТАКСИ́
3) ВЫ́ХОД
4) КО́ФЕ НЕТ
5) МУЗЕ́Й РУ́ССКИЙ

Basic contacts

6) Say 'Hello'.
7) Say 'Goodbye'.
8) Say 'Thank you'.
9) Say 'Excuse me'.
10) Say 'Thank you very much'.

Buying things

11) Ask how much it costs.
12) Say 'Three, please.'
13) Ask the assistant to show it to you.
14) Ask for two coffees.
15) Say 'Give me two postcards, please.'

How much is it?

16) Пять рубле́й.
17) Два рубля́ де́сять копе́ек.
18) Два́дцать рубле́й три́дцать шесть копе́ек.
19) Девяно́сто три копе́йки.
20) Со́рок де́вять рубле́й.

Asking for things in restaurants

21) Ask if there is tea.
22) Say 'What have you got?'
23) Ask for coffee without sugar.

24) Ask for mineral water.
25) Ask the waiter to bring the bill.

Getting around

26) Ask where the underground is.
27) Ask how to get there by transport.
28) Ask the passenger next to you to pass your **талóн** along to the ticket punch.
29) Ask the passenger in front of you if he is getting off.
30) Say 'Excuse me, where do I get off?'

Getting things done

31) Ask when the post-office (**пóчта**) opens.
32) Say 'Speak slowly, please.'
33) Say 'Do you speak English?'
34) Ask if you can order a taxi to the Bolshoy Theatre.
35) Say on the phone 'May I speak to Natasha?'

Work out the following times, days and telephone number

36) Приходи́те в семь часо́в.
37) Девятна́дцать часо́в три́дцать мину́т.
38) В сре́ду и в пя́тницу.
39) Ива́н Ива́нович бу́дет в четве́рг, у́тром.
40) Стó два́дцать три – шестьдеся́т вóсемь – нóль четы́ре.

Social encounters

41) Reply to Как вас зову́т?
42) Say 'Pleased to meet you.'
43) Say 'I like Moscow (or St Petersburg or the flat or Natasha) very much.'
44) Say 'Thank you. It was very tasty.'
45) Say 'Please give me your address (or telephone number).'

Answers to the exercises and test

Introduction

1 [spa-seé-ba] (Remember to pronounce unstressed **o** as [a])
   [dva kó-fye]
   [chye-tí-rye]
   [ya sloó-sha-yoo]
   [Gdye moo-zyéy?]
   [ma-ró-zhe-na-ye]
   [É-ta ha-ra-shó]
   [ón pree-dyót]
   [ta-vá-reeshsh]
   [dvye-ná-tsaty] (second **д** not audible)

2 **Signs:** [BAR] [BOO-FYÉT] [GA-STEÉ-NEE-TSA]
   [ZA-KRÍ-TA] [ZÁ-NYA-TA] [ZA-PRYE-SHSHYE-NÓ]
   [EEN-TOO-REÉST] [KÁ-SSA] [KSYE-BYÉ]
   [MYÉ-STA DLYA KOO-RYÉ-NEE-YA]
   [NYE KOO-REÉTY] [AT SYE-BYÁ]
   [PA-REEK-MÁ-HYER-SKA-YA] [PÓCH-TA]
   [RAZ-MYÉN] [RYE-MÓNT] [RYE-STA-RÁN]
   [SVA-BÓD-NA] [STÓP] [STA-YÁN-KA TAK-SEÉ]
   [TOO-A-LYÉT]

Unit 1

1 (a) [A-E-RA-FLÓT]
   (b) [VÓT-KA]
   (c) [EEN-TOO-REÉST]
   (d) [KEE-ÓSK]
   (e) [SANKT-PYE-TYER-BOÓRK]
   (f) [MASK-VÁ]
   (g) [PÉP-SEE-KÓ-LA]
   (h) [PRÁV-DA]

2 Здра́вствуйте, Ива́н Петро́вич.
   [Zdrá-stvooy-tye]

3 Здра́вствуй, Са́ша.
[Zdrá-stvooy]

4 Здра́вствуйте. Три ко́фе, пожа́луйста.
[Tree kó-fye, pa-zhál-sta]
Спаси́бо.
[Spa-sée-ba]

Оди́н чай, пожа́луйста.
[A-déen chay, pa-zhál-sta]
Спаси́бо.

5 (a) [a-déen], [dva], [tree], [chay], [kó-fye],
[chye-tí-rye], [spa-sée-ba], [pa-zhál-sta],
[Dó-bri dyeny], [Dó-bra-ye óo-tra],
[Da svee-dá-nee-ya], [Zdrá-stvooy-tye]
(b) [Mask-vá], [vót-ka], [Lón-dan], [Chay-kóf-skee],
[Da-sta-yéf-skee]
(c) Tolstoy (Толсто́й), Gorbachev (Горбачёв),
Pasternak (Пастерна́к), Solzhenitsyn
(Солжени́цын), Khrushchev (Хрущёв), Pushkin
(Пу́шкин), Prokofiev (Проко́фьев).

Unit 2

1 Four dollars.
2 Forty kopecks.
3 (a) Ско́лько сто́ит?
   (b) Три, пожа́луйста.
   (c) Два рубля́ де́сять копе́ек, пожа́луйста.
4 Ско́лько сто́ит (одна́) откры́тка?
Две, пожа́луйста.
Спаси́бо.
5 Ско́лько сто́ят я́блоки?
(А за) во́семь (рубле́й)?
Де́сять.
Хорошо́, оди́ннадцать.
Оди́н килогра́мм/Одно́ кило́.
6 Forty-four kopecks.
7 Sixty-six kopecks.
8 (a) Cashdesk
   (b) Apples 5 roubles a kilo
   (c) One postcard – 6 kopecks

Unit 3

1 Mineral water – no. Vodka – no. Black coffee – yes.
White coffee – no. Pepsi – no. Lemonade – yes.
(**сегóдня** 'today'; **у нас вóдки не бывáет** 'we
don't sell vodka')

2 A small coffee with sugar. (**Я возьмý чáшку** [Ya
vazy-moó chásh-koo] means 'I'll take a cup')

3 10 roubles 40 kopecks.

4 Официáнт, счёт, пожáлуйста.
Повторúте, пожáлуйста.

5 (a) 8 roubles 30 kopecks
  (b) 50 kopecks
  (c) 3 roubles 15 kopecks
  (d) 12 roubles 86 kopecks

6 Простúте, кóфе есть/есть кóфе?
Вóдка есть?
Чай есть?
Чтó (же) у вас есть?
Минерáльная водá, пожáлуйста.
Две, пожáлуйста. (бутьілка is feminine)

Unit 4

1 (a) on/to the right
  (b) on/to the left
  (c) straight on
  (d) (You have to) go (travel) three stops.

2 Простúте, где метрó?
Где останóвка?
Спасúбо.

3 (a) Простúте (or Скажúте), пожáлуйста, где
      гостúница Россúя?
  (b) Простúте, где метрó?
  (c) Простúте, как пройтú в Большóй теáтр?
  (d) Простúте, как проéхать тудá?

4 Простúте, где Крáсная плóщадь?
It's round the corner and straight on along the
street.

5 Нет (не выхожý).
You should get out of the way.

6 Простúте, где Эрмитáж?
Простúте, я не понимáю. Повторúте,

пожа́луйста.
А как прое́хать туда́?
Повтори́те, пожа́луйста.
Спаси́бо.

Unit 5

1 (a) Two o'clock/Two hours
   (b) 10pm (2200 hours)/Twenty-two hours
   (c) 6.30
   (d) The museum opens at 11.
   (e) The restaurant closes at 12.
   (f) On Wednesday
   (g) Come on Friday or Saturday.
   (h) Come on Thursday evening.

2 (a) 1300 (1pm)
   (b) 1201

3 (a) в суббо́ту
   (b) в три часа́
   (c) ве́чером
   (d) за́втра
   (e) за́втра ве́чером

4 M/W/F   9 a.m. – 1 p.m.
   Tu/Th/Sa   2 p.m. – 6 p.m.

5 (a) 256-02-35
   (b) 125-70-99

6 Прости́те (Скажи́те), пожа́луйста, когда́
   открыва́ется музе́й
   Повтори́те, пожа́луйста.
   А когда́ о́н (masculine) закрыва́ется?
   Спаси́бо.

7 Здра́вствуйте. Мо́жно заказа́ть такси́?
   Сего́дня ве́чером.
   Во́семь часо́в.
   В рестора́н Узбекиста́н.

8 Позови́те, пожа́луйста, Ната́шу.
   (She's not here at the moment.)
   Говори́те ме́дленно, пожа́луйста. Я
   иностра́нец/иностра́нка.
   (She's not here. She'll come about eight.)
   Повтори́те, пожа́луйста.
   (She'll come at eight o'clock.)
   Хорошо́, я перезвоню́ в во́семь (часо́в).

Unit 6

1 (a) Меня́ зову́т...
(b) Как вас зову́т?

2 (a) Irina Nikolaevna [Ee-ree-na Nee-ka-lá-yev-na]
(b) Tatyana Aleksandrovna [Ta-tyyá-na A-lyek-sán-drav-na]

3 О́чень прия́тно.
О́чень.

4 Пожа́луйста *or* Нет, спаси́бо.
Нет, спаси́бо, я сыт(á).
Спаси́бо, (я) не могу́.

5 To our friendship, to the English (British) people.

6 За мир/за дру́жбу/за англо-ру́сскую дру́жбу/
за вас/за нас/за Ната́шу (accusative case –
see Unit 5 note 7).

'Can you get by?'

1) [RYE-STA-RÁN] RESTAURANT
2) [TAK-SÉE] TAXI
3) [VÍ-HAT] EXIT
4) [KÓ-FYE NYET] NO COFFEE
5) [ROO-SKEE MOO-ZYÉY] RUSSIAN MUSEUM
6) Здра́вствуйте.
7) До свида́ния.
8) Спаси́бо.
9) Прости́те.
10) Спаси́бо большо́е.
11) Ско́лько (э́то) сто́ит?
12) Три, пожа́луйста.
13) Покажи́те (э́то), пожа́луйста.
14) Два ко́фе, пожа́луйста.
15) (Да́йте) две откры́тки, пожа́луйста.
16) 5 roubles.
17) 2 roubles 10 kopecks.
18) 20 roubles 36 kopecks.
19) 93 kopecks.
20) 49 roubles.
21) Чай есть?

22) Что́ у вас есть?
23) Ко́фе без са́хара, пожа́луйста.
24) Минера́льная вода́, пожа́луйста.
25) (Официа́нт), счёт, пожа́луйста.
26) (Прости́те), где метро́?
27) Как прое́хать туда́?
28) Переда́йте тало́н, пожа́луйста.
29) Вы выхо́дите?
30) Прости́те, где (мне) выходи́ть?
31) Когда́ открыва́ется по́чта?
32) Говори́те ме́дленно, пожа́луйста.
33) Вы говори́те по-англи́йски?
34) Мо́жно заказа́ть такси́ в Большо́й теа́тр?
35) Позови́те, пожа́луйста, Ната́шу.
36) Come at 7.
37) 1930 (7.30pm).
38) On Wednesday and Friday.
39) Ivan Ivanovich will be (here) on Thursday, in the morning.
40) 123-68-04.
41) Меня́ зову́т (your name).
42) О́чень прия́тно.
43) Мне о́чень нра́вится Москва́/(Санкт-) Петербу́рг/кварти́ра/Ната́ша.
44) Спаси́бо. Бы́ло о́чень вку́сно.
45) Да́йте (or Скажи́те), пожа́луйста, ваш а́дрес/телефо́н.

Word list (Russian-English)

Quick reference alphabet in dictionary order

А	Б	В	Г	Д	Е	Ё	Ж	З	И	Й	К	Л	М	Н	О	П	Р
а	б	в	г	д	е	ё	ж	з	и	й	к	л	м	н	о	п	р
a	b	v	g	d	ye	yo	zh	z	ee	y	k	l	m	n	o	p	r

С	Т	У	Ф	Х	Ц	Ч	Ш	Щ	Ъ	Ы	Ь	Э	Ю	Я
с	т	у	ф	х	ц	ч	ш	щ	ъ	ы	ь	э	ю	я
s	t	oo	f	h	ts	ch	sh	shsh	–	i	y	e	yoo	ya

This vocabulary list gives all the vocabulary used in the conversations and exercises. The number shows the unit in which the word first occurs. Pronunciation is shown only when there is some exceptional feature

а 2	*but/and*
автобус 4	*bus*
áдрес 6	*address*
аллё! 5	*hello (on phone)*
английский 6	*English/British*
Áнглия 2	*England/Britain*
апельсиновый сок 3	*orange juice*
аспирин 1	*aspirin*
бáбушка 6	*grandmother*
без 3	*without*
без сáхара 3	*without sugar*
бéлое винó 3	*white wine*
берúйте 6	*do take some*
билéт 2	*ticket*
большóй 3	*large, big*
бóрщ 3	*beetroot soup*
брат 6	*brother*
(óн) бýдет 5	*(he) will (be)*
(вы) бýдете 3	*(you) will*
бýдьте добры 3	*be so good/excuse me*
бутербрóд 3	*open sandwich*
бутербрóд с сыром 3	*cheese sandwich*
бутылка 3	*bottle*
было 6	*(it) was*
в 4/5	*in/to/at*
вам 3	*to you/for you*
вас 1	*you (accusative of вы)*

ваш 5	your
ва́ше 6	your
ва́ше здоро́вье! 6	your health!
ва́ши 2	your (plural of ваш)
вегетариа́нец 3	vegetarian
ве́чер 1	evening
ве́чером 5	in the evening
вино́ 3	wine
вку́сно 6	tasty
вода́ 3	water
во́дка 3	vodka
во́семь 2	eight
во́семьдесят 2	eighty
воскресе́нье 5	Sunday
вот 2	here/there (pointing)
вре́мя 5	time
всего́ [fsye-vó] 2	altogether/in all
вто́рник 5	Tuesday
второ́е блю́до 3	second (main) course
вхо́д 4	entrance
вчера́ 5	yesterday
вы 3	you
вы́пить 3	to drink (alcohol)
вы́ход 4	exit
(вы) выхо́дите 4	(you) are getting out
выходи́ть 4	to get out
(я) выхожу́ 4	(I) am getting out
где 4	where
(вы) говори́те 5	(you) speak
говори́те ме́дленно 5	speak slowly
го́род 6	city/town
гру́ши 2	pears
да 2	yes
дава́йте вы́пьем 6	let's drink
да́йте 5	give (me)
далеко́ 4	far
два 1	two
два́дцать 2	twenty
двена́дцать 2	twelve
две́сти 5	two hundred
девяно́сто 2	ninety
де́вять 2	nine
де́душка 6	grandfather
день 5	day
десе́рт 3	dessert
де́сять 2	ten
для 3	for
для вас 3	for you
до 4	as far as/until

до за́втра 6	*see you tomorrow*
до свида́ния 1	*goodbye*
добра́ться [da-brá-tsa] 4	*to reach/get to*
до́брый 1	*good/kind*
договори́лись 5	*that's agreed/OK*
до́ллар 2	*dollar*
до́м 6	*house/building*
дороги́е 6	*(my) dears*
до́рого 2	*expensive*
до́чь 6	*daughter*
дру́жба 6	*friendship*
его́ [ye-vó] 5	*him/of him*
её 5	*her/of her*
(я) ем 3	*(I) eat*
е́сли 2	*if*
есть 3	*to eat*
есть 3	*is/are*
есть? 3	*is there?*
ещё раз 2	*again*
жена́ 6	*wife*
жена́т 6	*married (of man)*
(вы) живёте 6	*(you) live*
за 2	*for*
за знако́мство 6	*to our meeting*
за нас 6	*to us*
за угло́м 4	*round the corner*
за́втра 5	*tomorrow*
за́втра у́тром 5	*tomorrow morning*
зака́з 5	*order*
заказа́ть 5	*to order*
закрыва́ется 5	*closes*
замеча́тельно 6	*marvellous*
за́мужем 6	*married (of woman)*
за́нят 5	*busy (man)*
занята́ 5	*busy (woman)*
(я) запишу́ 6	*(I')ll write (it) down*
здесь 4	*here*
здоро́вье 6	*health*
здра́вствуй 1	*hello (informal)*
здра́вствуйте 1	*hello*
(вы) зна́ете 4	*(you) know*
(я) зна́ю 3	*(I) know*
зову́т 6	*(they) call*
и 2	*and*
извини́те 4	*excuse (me)*
и́ли 3	*either/or*
и́мя 6	*first name*
иностра́нец 5	*foreigner (man)*

иностра́нка 5	*foreigner (woman)*
к нам 5	*to us*
к сожале́нию 6	*unfortunately*
ка́ждый 5	*every*
как 4	*how*
как вас зову́т? 6	*what's your name?*
как прое́хать ...? 4	*How do I get to ... (by transport)?*
как пройти́...? 4	*How do I get to... (on foot)?*
како́й 3	*what kind of*
ка́сса 2	*cash desk/ticket office*
кварти́ра 6	*flat*
кило́ 2	*kilo*
килогра́мм 2	*kilogram*
когда́ 4	*when*
колбаса́ 3	*salami*
конве́рт 2	*envelope*
коне́чно 5 [ka-nyésh-na]	*of course*
копе́йка 2	*kopeck*
ко́рпус 6	*block*
ко́фе 1	*coffee*
Кра́сная пло́щадь 4	*Red Square*
кра́сное вино́ 3	*red wine*
кро́ме 5	*except*
куда́ 5	*(to) where*
лу́чше [loó-che] 4	*better*
ма́ленький 3	*small*
ме́дленно 5	*slowly*
меню́ 3	*menu*
меня́ 5	*me*
меня́ зову́т... 6	*my name is...*
метро́ 4	*metro/underground*
ми́лости про́сим 6	*welcome*
минера́льная вода́ 3	*mineral water*
мину́та 5	*minute*
мир 6	*peace*
мир на земле́ 6	*peace on earth*
мне 2	*for me/to me*
мне на́до 4	*I have to*
(я) могу́ 5	*(I) can*
мо́жно 2	*it's possible*
мой 6	*my*
моро́женое 3	*ice cream*
муж 6	*husband*
музе́й 4	*museum*
на 4	*on/to*
на второ́е 3	*for the main course*
на десе́рт 3	*for dessert*
на здоро́вье 6	*may it do you good*

на́до 4	it is necessary
нале́во 4	on/to the left
нали́ть ещё? 6	can I pour some more?
напра́во 4	on/to the right
на́ша 6	our
не 3	not
не́ за что 4	don't mention it
не кладите тру́бку 5	don't hang up
не нра́вится... 6	I don't like...
недалеко́ 4	not far
нельзя́ 5	it's not possible
нет 2	no
нет 3	there is no
не́ту (colloquial) 3	there is no
неча́янно 5	accidentally
ничего́ [nee-chye-vó] 5	it doesn't matter
но́ль 5	zero
но́мер 4	number
нра́вится 6	(it) pleases
обяза́тельно 6	definitely
о́вощи 3	vegetables
оди́н 1	one
оди́ннадцать 2	eleven
одну́ мину́ту 3	just a minute
о́й! 2	oh!
о́н 4	he
она́ 5	she
остано́вка 4	stop
открыва́ется 5	opens
откры́тка 2	postcard
отсю́да 4	from here
о́тчество 6	patronymic
официа́нт 3	waiter/waitress
о́чень 2	very/very much
о́чень прия́тно 6	pleased to meet you
переда́йте 4	pass (this) along
(я) перезвоню́ 5	(I')ll ring back
пи́во 3	beer
письмо́ 2	letter
пить 3	to drink
пло́щадь 4	square
по 4	along
по у́лице 4	along the street
по-англи́йски 5	in English
повтори́ 6	repeat (familiar)
повтори́те 2	repeat
(вы) пое́дете 5	(you) will go
пожа́луйста 1	please/don't mention it/please do/here you are

позвони́те 6	ring/telephone
(я) позвоню́ 6	(I')ll phone
познако́мьтесь 6	let me introduce you
позови́те 5	call
пока́ 6	see you soon
покажи́те 2	show (me)
понеде́льник 5	Monday
(я) понима́ю 5	(I) understand
(нам) пора́ уходи́ть 6	it's time (for us) to go
посла́ть 2	to send
по́чта 4	post office
(о́н) придёт 5	(he) will come
(я) принесу́ 3	(I')ll bring
приходи́те 5	come
прия́тно 6	pleasant
проспе́кт 4	avenue
прости́те 1	excuse (me)
про́сто 6	simply
проходи́те 6	come/go through
пря́мо 4	straight on
пя́тница 5	Friday
пять 2	five
пятьдеся́т 2	fifty
рабо́тает 5	works
разбуди́ть 5	to wake
(я вас) разбужу́ 5	(I')ll wake (you)
раздева́йтесь 6	take off your coat
рубль 2	rouble
ру́сский 4	Russian
ры́ба 3	fish
ря́дом 4	nearby/alongside
с 3	with
с вас 3	from you/you owe
сади́тесь 4	get in/sit down
самолётом 2	by plane
са́хар 3	sugar
сего́дня 5 [sye-vód-nya]	today
сего́дня ве́чером 5	this evening
сейча́с 5	now/right now
семь 2	seven
се́мьдесят 2	seventy
сестра́ 6	sister
сесть 4	to sit/take transport
скажи́те 2	tell (me)
ско́лько 2	how much/how many
ско́лько сто́ит? 2	how much does it cost?
ско́лько сто́ят? 2	how much do they cost
сле́дующая остано́вка 4	the next stop
(я) слу́шаю 1	I'm listening
со́к 3	juice

со́рок 2	forty
спаси́бо 1	thank you
спаси́бо большо́е 2	thank you very much
среда́ 5	Wednesday
сто́ 2	hundred
сто́имость зака́за 5	the cost of the order
сто́ит 2	costs
Столи́чная во́дка 2	Stolichnaya vodka
суббо́та 5	Saturday
сухо́е вино́ 3	dry wine
сча́стье [shshá-styye] 6	happiness
счёт [shshyot] 3	bill
сын 6	son
сыр 3	cheese
(я) сыт (man) 6	I can't eat any more
(я) сыта́ (woman) 6	I can't eat any more
так 2	so
такси́ 4	taxi
тало́н 4	travel coupon/ticket
та́почки 6	slippers
теа́тр 4	theatre
телефо́н 5	telephone/phone number
това́рищ 6	comrade
тогда́ 3	then
то́же 3	too
то́лько 3	only
то́чное вре́мя 5	exact time
трамва́й 4	tram
три 1	three
три́дцать 2	thirty
тролле́йбус 4	trolleybus
тру́бка 5	receiver
туда́ 4	(to) there
ты 6	you (familiar)
у вас 3	you have
у вас есть...? 3	have you got...?
у́лица 4	street
у́тро 1	morning
у́тром 5	in the morning
(я) хочу́ 2	(I) want
фами́лия 6	surname
хорошо́ 2	good/well/OK
чай 1	tea
час 5	hour
че́рез час 5	in an hour
четве́рг 5	Thursday
четы́ре 1	four

что 3 [shtó]		what
что же 3 [shtó zhe]		what (more emphatic)
шесть 2		six
шестьдеся́т 2		sixty
Эрмита́ж 4		the Hermitage
э́то 2		this/that/it
я 1		I
я́блоки 2		apples

Selected English-Russian phrase list

English	Russian
Does anyone here speak English?	**Кто здесь говори́т по-англи́йски?** [Któ zdyesy ga-va-ree't pa-an-glee'-skee?]
Doctor	**До́ктор** [Dók-tar]
Excuse me	**Прости́те** [Pra-stee'-tye]
Go away	**Уходи́те** [Oo-ha-dee'-tye]
Help me, please	**Помоги́те, пожа́луйста** [Pa-ma-gee'-tye, pa-zhál-sta]
Repeat, please	**Повтори́те, пожа́луйста** [Pa-fta-ree'-tye, pa-zhál-sta]
Write it down please	**Напиши́те, пожа́луйста** [Na-pee-shi'-tye, pa-zhál-sta]
I'm English	**Я англича́нин** (man) [Ya an-glee-chá-neen]
	англича́нка (woman) an-glee-chán-ka]
Irish	**ирла́ндец** (man) eer-lán-dyets]
	ирла́ндка (woman) eer-lánt-ka]
Scottish	**шотла́ндец** (man) shat-lán-dyets]
	шотла́ндка (woman) shat-lánt-ka]
Welsh	**валли́ец** (man) va-lee'-yets]
	валли́йка (woman) va-lee'-ka]

Further study

Dictionary

A very good and inexpensive dictionary is *The Pocket Oxford Russian-English English-Russian Dictionary*, Oxford University Press, 1981.

Further study

If you want to study Russian in more detail, including all the basic grammar, there is N.J. Brown, *Russian in Three Months*, Hugo's Language Books, 1988. Fourth impression 1992. A more demanding course is Harrison, Clarkson and Le Fleming, *Colloquial Russian*, Routledge, 1973.

The Centre for Information on Language Teaching (CILT) has information on all the Russian teaching materials in print in Britain. Their offices and library are at Regent's College, Inner Circle, Regent's Park, London NW1 4NS. Tel: 071-486 8221.